Dance

as a Way of Knowing

JENNIFER DONOHUE ZAKKAI

Stenhouse Publishers

The Galef Institute

Strategies for Teaching and Learning Professional Library

Look for announcements of future titles in this series on science and visual arts.

Stenhouse Publishers, 431 York Street, York, Maine 03909
The Galef Institute, 11050 Santa Monica Boulevard, Third Floor, Los Angeles, California 90025

Library of Congress Cataloging-in-Publication Data
Zakkai, Jennifer Donohue.
    Dance as a way of knowing / Jennifer Donohue Zakkai.
      p. cm.
    Includes bibliographical references.
    ISBN 1-57110-064-4 (alk. paper)
    1. Dance—Study and teaching. 2. Movement education.
    3. Interdisciplinary approach in education. 4. Learning.
    I. Title.
    GV1589.Z35 1997
    792.8—dc21
                                       97-29629
                                         CIP

Manufactured in the United States of America on acid-free paper.
00 99 98 97 8 7 6 5 4 3 2 1

Dear Colleague,

The extraordinary resource books in this series support our common goal as educators to apply best practices to everyday teaching. These books will encourage you to examine new resources and to discover and try out new and different teaching strategies. We hope you'll want to discuss and reflect on your strategies with other teachers and coaches in your support study group meetings (both face-to-face and virtual) to make the most of the rich learning and teaching opportunities each discipline offers.

If we truly believe that all children can be successful in school, then we must find ways to help all children develop to their full potential. This requires an understanding of how children learn, thoughtful preparation of curriculum, continuous reflection, adaptation of everyday practices, and ongoing professional support. To that end, the *Strategies for Teaching and Learning Professional Library* was developed. The series offers you countless opportunities for professional growth. It's rather like having your own workshops, coaching, and study groups between the covers of a book.

Each book in this series invites you to explore
   • the theory regarding human learning and development—so you know why,
   • the best instructional practices—so you know how, and
   • continuous assessment of your students' learning as well as your own teaching and understanding—so you and your students know that you know.

The books offer *Dialogues* to reflect upon your practices, on your own and in study groups. The Dialogues invite responses to self-evaluative questions, and encourage experimentation with new instructional strategies.

Shoptalks provide short, lively reviews of the best and latest professional literature as well as professional journals and associations.

Teacher-To-Teacher Field Notes are full of tips and experiences from other practicing educators who offer different ways of thinking about teaching practices and a wide range of successful, practical classroom strategies and techniques to draw upon.

It's our hope that as you explore and reflect on your teaching practice, you'll continue to expand your teaching repertoire and share your success with your colleagues.

Sincerely,

Linda Adelman Johannesen

Linda Adelman Johannesen
President
The Galef Institute

The Strategies for Teaching and Learning Professional Library is part of the Galef Institute's school reform initiative *Different Ways of Knowing.*

Different Ways of Knowing is a philosophy of education based on research in child development, cognitive theory, and multiple intelligences. It offers teachers, administrators, artists and other specialists, and other school and district educators continuing professional growth opportunities integrated with teaching and learning materials. The materials are supportive of culturally and linguistically diverse school populations and help all teachers and children to be successful. Teaching strategies focus on interdisciplinary, thematic instruction integrating history and social studies with the performing and visual arts, literature, writing, math, and science. Developed with the leadership of Senior Author Linda Adelman Johannesen, *Different Ways of Knowing* has been field tested in hundreds of classrooms across the country.

For more information, contact

The Galef Institute
11050 Santa Monica Boulevard, Third Floor, Los Angeles, California 90025
Tel 310.479.8883
Fax 310.473.9720
www.dwoknet.galef.org

Strategies for Teaching and Learning Professional Library

Contributors

President
Linda Adelman Johannesen

Senior Vice President
Sue Beauregard

Editors
Resa Gabe Nikol
Susan Zinner

Designer
Delfina Marquez-Noé

Photographers
Ted Beauregard
Dana Ross

I thank the following educators for contributing their strategies and insights: Ron Aschieris, Nancy Gates, Char Girard, Richard Jacobsen, Maureen Manning, Nan Mohr, Dan Montoya, Donna Schmidt, Pam Strain, Mary Tappan, Laura Gray, Terry Gogol, Judy Singleton, and Debbra Lang.

I thank my colleagues in dance and education for their generosity and guidance, especially Diana Cummins who supplied resources and support throughout my writing process, as well as Susan Cambigue-Tracey, W. Rex Comer, Jean Miller McComb, Jane Remer, Patty Yancey, Victoria Marks, Sophiline Cheam Shapiro, Jessica Nicoll, Rose Ann Thom, Jo Anne Bailey, and Gregory Acker.

At the Galef Institute, my gratitude goes to Karolynne Gee for helping me understand how learners of all ages construct and communicate meaning. I appreciate the work of my editor, Resa Gabe Nikol, who shepherded this book from start to finish with respect and insight.

For their participation in the photo shoot for the book, I thank Skye Aldrin, Natalie Foster, India Rae Hawkins, Adriana Jauregui, Raphael and Magaly Lopez, Adreene and Alerissa Mariano, Carrie Plumridge, Meljon Salazar, and dancer Madeleine Dahm. Thanks, also, to Devora Kaye.

Finally, I must acknowledge Bessie Schönberg, Don Redlich, and Billy Siegenfeld—whose gifts as artists and educators inspired my approach to learning and creating in dance. —JDZ

Special thanks to Andrew G. Galef and Bronya Pereira Galef for their continuing commitment to our nation's children and educators.

Contents

Chapter 1
Moving To Learn

Every day young people dance into classrooms to learn. They drift, scamper, and race into their chairs. Once seated, they're apt to swing their legs, tap rhythmically on tabletops, and gaze around the room—often with lightning speed. They never seem to stop moving.

Children, after all, are used to experiencing life through motion. From infancy, they learn by physically interacting with their environment. They investigate objects through touch, and crawl through living spaces like world explorers. After much experimentation, they stand, balance, and walk. Soon their repertoire expands to running, hopping, skipping, and twirling.

Until they master spoken language, children depend on a variety of gestures to express their needs and responses to the world around them. Perhaps you've witnessed a child echo the beat of some lively music, or act out a story with friends. In many ways, full-bodied movement is the medium through which children express the vivid intentions of their own imaginations.

Full-bodied, expressive movement is also the medium through which cultures and individuals have communicated their beliefs, values, and artistic visions throughout time. Children, then, are innately primed to learn and share what they know through dance.

As adults, however, we are less fluent with vibrant movement. In the classroom, students' irrepressible energy can rise up like a wave that threatens to push us away from our teaching goals. Our impulse is to stifle this energy, and there seem to be good reasons to do so—children need to learn to concentrate and control their actions. But as first-grade teacher Dan Montoya from Emma W. Shuey Elementary School in Rosemead, California, says, "Instead of putting a lid on our students' energy, we can channel it." Montoya and his colleagues participated in teacher workshops that demonstrated how learners of all ages build on natural movements to explore concepts, solve creative problems, and communicate ideas across the curriculum.

A Workshop on Paper

If you seek to channel your students' vitality into meaningful learning experiences, consider this book your very own "workshop on paper." *Dance as a Way of Knowing* is designed to build on your knowledge of movement and dance and provide strategies you can use to enhance students' learning and creativity in the classroom.

Children are used to experiencing life through motion.

The good news is that you do not have to be a skilled mover to be an effective facilitator of movement. You'll use verbal directions to guide most movement activities. That's because our goal is to cultivate children's creativity, not teach them a particular way to move. We want our students to investigate and develop their own movement ideas, not imitate us or others.

Let's dispel a myth about working with movement and dance. It is not an unstructured experience. Students enjoy solving very specific, challenging movement problems that require the utmost concentration and inspire a high level of personal expression.

An Introduction to Movement and Dance
To understand how movement and dance can enhance children's learning, let's visit three teachers at Emma W. Shuey Elementary School in Rosemead, California, as they incorporate movement activities in their classrooms.

Donna Schmidt is helping her kindergartners understand the shape of alphabet letters. Holding a wide piece of ribbon straight up and down, she asks students to show her this shape with their hands and whole bodies. A forest of different vertical lines appear before her. Schmidt turns the ribbon on its side to make a horizontal straight line and asks her students to show her this line through different body shapes. Next, her students will put vertical and horizontal lines together to form the letter "L," as well as other straight-lined letter shapes. Later, they can transfer their knowledge of straight lines when they investigate geometric shapes through movement.

Nan Mohr has invited her fifth-grade students to explore the impact of the moon's gravity on oceans. They stand together in pairs, about four feet apart, holding an imaginary rope between them. One student pulls on the rope while the other student is pulled toward him. They reverse roles and explore this back-and-forth motion several times. Then students put the rope aside and are asked to imagine invisible connections anywhere but between their hands and arms. They are guided to make their actions larger and stronger. Students discover a variety of pulling and "being-pulled" movements that help them understand the *effect* the moon causes in ocean tides.

Maureen Manning and her fourth graders have created a dance to present at a school assembly. It is based on a magical tale they wrote together about a special place where inhabitants flourish as learners—the "Land of Rosanbeek."

Manning has learned how to help her students discover and refine their inventive movements. The result of everyone's efforts is a dynamic and original dance. While a student narrates from the side of the stage, music plays over the auditorium's speakers. Dancers appear as powerful creatures, and stalk across the stage against a colorful painted backdrop. With fluid movements, they stretch their arms into space, then curve their backs quickly and sharply, communicating the nature of these mysterious creatures to the hushed audience.

You can see that movement and dance is integral to learning—from exploring a curriculum topic, such as letter shapes, or concept, such as cause and effect, to making a dance. The terms "movement and dance" encompass a full range of motion—from the movement that exists in the natural and human-made worlds around us, to everyday actions we all engage in as human beings, to the carefully crafted movements we know as dance. *Dance as a Way of Knowing* describes how this full spectrum of movement enhances classroom learning.

To that end, "movement and dance" is used as an umbrella term for the whole progression of strategies offered in this book. Since everyday actions are used as a starting point, referring to all the experiences as "dance" is not accurate. On the other hand, "movement" cannot account for students' emerging creative expression as they learn more about dance and incorporate aesthetic elements into their movement choices.

The Benefits of Movement and Dance

The benefits of inviting students to work with movement and dance are numerous and far-reaching. Movement and dance helps students

- focus and engage in learning
- apply their kinesthetic intelligence
- understand concepts and themes
- develop and refine their higher level thinking skills
- communicate in unique ways and appreciate the artistic expression of others
- develop spatial awareness
- cooperate and collaborate with each other.

Focus and Engage in Learning

Maureen Manning and her fourth graders start each day with movement. She believes it focuses and prepares them to learn. "Their brains are alive and alert. They become excited about what they are going to do next," she reported to me recently.

It's easy to understand why. Having to sit still for long stretches of time can actually create tension in some children. Others carry with them the stresses of their lives outside the classroom. Moving the whole body improves circulation and sends oxygen to the brain. It also releases endorphins which ease stress and promote a sense of well-being.

In movement and dance experiences, students always work with specific points of focus as they move. They might be asked to walk at different speeds, respond to a dynamic piece of music, or explore geometric shapes through movement. Because they are focusing their minds as well as their movements, they experience an immediate and simultaneous fusion of intention, action, feeling, and awareness. Psychologist Mihaly Csikszentmihalyi (1993) refers to this kind of completely absorbing and pleasurable concentration as "optimal flow experience."

It's been my experience that total engagement can make learning deep and memorable. In this way, moving to learn can be highly motivating and have long-lasting impact.

A Tool for Learning

Recently I conducted a workshop in Bloomfield Hills, Michigan, to help educators understand how movement and dance could be integrated into classroom learning. Debbra Lang, Executive Director for Instruction, later commented that the workshop had demonstrated "how the arts demand a rethinking of how we apply information. It wasn't just moving, it was translating information into movement."

Because students are focusing their minds as well as their movements, they experience an immediate and simultaneous fusion of intention, action, feeling, and awareness.

Author and educator Howard Gardner (1983, 1993) proposes that all human beings have multiple intelligences. He has identified at least seven—logical-mathematical, linguistic, spatial, bodily-kinesthetic, musical, interpersonal, and intrapersonal—which we use to acquire knowledge and demonstrate what we know. Together with more traditional ways of receiving, recording, and reflecting knowledge, students can also use their bodily-kinesthetic intelligence to learn and show what they know about different topics, concepts, and processes through movement.

For example, in language arts, we can put action words into motion to reinforce and demonstrate comprehension. Let's see how this would work. Begin by reading this paragraph:

> Human beings are in constant motion. Even when we sit completely still, lost in thought, our hearts are pumping, our lungs are expanding and contracting, our chests rise and fall. Soon we blink, shift our weight, unclasp our hands, turn our heads, stand up, and walk across the room.

Now, let's highlight the action words. Move your hands and create your own way of understanding what we mean by *expand, contract, rise, fall,* and *walk.*

Give this a try with your students. You'll discover that they'll enjoy exploring the meaning of action words from any text with their hands and whole bodies.

Students studying earth science can investigate the role volcanos play in changing the earth's surface, and explore key concepts through movement. Students use their bodies to learn how pressure builds underground and forces magma out of the earth, and how lava flows in rivers down mountainsides and forms rock. The information they study in their reference books, through slides, or video, comes to life through their movement experience.

A vital connection exists between cursive writing and movement. First students draw big, free-form continuous curving lines on an imaginary surface all around themselves. They concentrate on the curves that make up cursive writing such as loops, under and over curves, and circles. Then they are ready to put these shapes together and write words in cursive motion on an imaginary chalkboard in front of them. Writing correctly formed, curved letters that flow together through gross motor movements can help students meet the fine motor challenges of writing in cursive on paper.

Field Notes: Teacher-To-Teacher

I find that as my third graders learn the shapes of cursive letters, they seem to learn more quickly and retain the letter forms when I ask them to form the letters using their arms, legs, and bodies. Then we skywrite the letters with our pointed fingers. Later, when my students write the cursive letters on paper, they are better able to visualize each letter form and duplicate it. They also seem better able to mentally reproduce and retain the proper lines and sequences following this combination of creative movement and writing practice.

Mary Tappan
Mildred B. Janson Elementary School
Rosemead, California

Acknowledging the Kinesthetic Learner

It's hard to imagine a classroom without several individuals in perpetual motion. They are the ones who squirm in their chairs and jiggle anything with moving parts. They are the first to volunteer to get equipment from the school office. They don't simply walk—they burst into a room. They jump and touch any hanging object within three feet of their fingertips. They live for recess.

Although we may label these students as "hyper" and view them as troublesome, we would do well to look at school through their eyes. They may be trying to tell us that they have a strong bodily-kinesthetic intelligence. We can help them focus it on learning.

One morning, while facilitating a series of movement lessons with a K-2 class at the Elizabeth Street School in Cudahy, California, I asked students to explore straight lines and curved lines. Using our bodies, we put the lines together to create letters of the alphabet. From the moment we began our first lesson, it was clear that Joseph loved to move. He stood right in front of me, his body bristling with energy, his eyes gleaming with pleasure. He listened attentively and made accurate, inventive choices. The straight lines he created with his arms and legs were long and firm. Often he bent over at an angle or balanced on one leg to find unusual ways of making straight lines.

While exploring curved shapes, he waved me over and whispered, "I am an egg." Indeed, he was not round like a orange, but arched in an oval shape. He was able to sense the shape he was making and connect it to an existing object.

When the class reflected at the end of the lesson, Joseph was able to label nearly every kind of movement he had experienced. He could also identify the letters we had covered. After class, his teacher, Terry Gogol, mentioned how surprised and delighted she was with Joseph's participation. She explained that he was a new arrival to the class, could hardly read, and was often severely disruptive. Learning through moving is highly motivating for children like Joseph. The success they experience as creative movers can help them access other skills.

When English Is a Second Language

Second language learners can understand the meaning of words through movement. A movement lesson is a perfect opportunity to build students' basic vocabulary. As they label all the different ways the body can move, students learn action words like *stretch, turn, skip*. They also discover such spatial concepts as *high, low, circular.* Adverbs—*lightly, powerfully, quickly*—come to life as well. Second language learners who are not yet speaking and writing in English will appreciate movement as a way to learn and demonstrate what they know.

Field Notes: Teacher-To-Teacher

Each year I have students who know they are not successful in school. They may not read and write as well as others. Or their English is not as sharp because they recently emigrated from another country. This doesn't mean, however, that they don't understand the concepts we are exploring in our classroom. Ten-year-old Clifford knew that he could use his body to show us what he knew. When he created physical sequences to demonstrate the movement of a wave, he experienced success through movement and developed the confidence to work on his reading, writing, and speaking. Other students have shown me what they know about diverse concepts—molecular structure, social organization, and the causes of war, to name a few.

Nan Mohr
Emma W. Shuey Elementary School
Rosemead, California

Second language learners who are not yet speaking and writing in English, will appreciate movement as a way to learn and demonstrate what they know.

Higher Level Thinking Skills

Movement and dance experiences develop students' high-level thinking skills by engaging them in exploration, creative problem solving, and decision-making.

Exploration. Students learn about the key components of dance through *movement exploration*. Movement exploration, which I'll describe in more detail in later chapters, involves students in a structured yet open-ended process of investigation. Students discover inventive movements as they explore specific dance ideas.

Creative problem solving. The ability to confront a problem and discover a creative solution is one of our most powerful resources. All inventions, advances in science, emerging artistic styles, helpful new products and services, even new understandings about how people learn, have been created by individuals who identified a need, envisioned a way to fulfill that need, then took the necessary steps to find a solution.

Each of us is creative. But creativity is like a muscle. We need to use and exercise our creativity so that we can develop it and make it strong. Whether we are designing an invention, sculpting clay, or solving a community problem, we benefit from knowing there is more than one way to achieve a goal.

Movement and dance encourages students to explore a variety of solutions to a movement problem. Once they realize there is not just one right answer, but a range of more and less effective choices, students are inspired to take greater risks and invest themselves more deeply as learners. As they learn new skills and discover that their individual choices have value, they can grow in their self-confidence and productivity.

Decision-making. To coalesce their learning, students are asked to create sequences of movement which can range from simple juxtapositions to a complete dance. Selecting, sequencing, and revising their movement choices into a whole asks them to think with discernment as they transform movement into effective communication.

Dance Is a Unique Form of Communication

Working creatively can develop our thinking skills and empower us as individuals. Our lives are also enhanced when we experience the artistic expression of others—such as a dance, musical composition, or painting.

We participate in a special kind of human communication in which we speak the same language even though no words are exchanged. Sometimes artists invite us to look at people, issues, and designs through a "different lens." This process can be so powerful that we enlarge or dramatically alter the way we view ourselves and others who may have lives completely different from our own.

Therefore, it is important that students not only learn how to communicate their ideas through movement and dance, but also learn to experience the kinesthetic expressions of others as observers. As students view each other's efforts as well as the work of dance artists, they can develop their aesthetic awareness and critical thinking skills. This learning can sharpen their assessment of their own work and inspire them to a higher level of achievement.

Investigating dances from different times and cultures can offer students a different way to know a historical era or group of people. For instance, students can investigate how Africans held on to their cultural and spiritual identity through their music and dances when they were forced to disperse throughout the world because of slavery. Then students can trace the profound impact African music and dance have had on music and dance in North America, the Caribbean, and South America.

To learn more about dance, invite artists and dance groups in your community, or those who travel and teach throughout the United States, to perform and work with you. This way, students can reach outside their immediate environment and extend their learning into a larger artistic community.

Spatial Awareness

To work with movement and dance successfully, students need to become aware of the space they are moving in, their personal space, and the space of others. Students find it both challenging and enjoyable to learn how to move freely without bumping into anyone.

No matter how large or small the workspace, students can learn to move within clearly defined parameters. Depending on their age, they use concrete images in a movement lesson, like a bubble or a spaceship, to focus on the area slightly larger than their fully extended bodies—their personal space. Whether moving in place or traveling through space, they will look where they are going and remain sensitive to the parameters of their personal space and that of others.

Spatial awareness has enormous benefits. Rambunctious students develop more self-control and respect for others, while quieter students feel it's safe to move and take risks. Then as the facilitator, you can concentrate on how students are moving, rather than on traffic problems.

Cooperation and Collaboration

While movement and dance experiences emphasize individual expression, students are also constantly working with each other, either as fellow movers or collaborators. In the beginning, students explore movement problems as a whole group, since it takes a while for everyone to get familiar with this new way of learning. Later, they break into smaller groups to share their ideas and solve problems together. As viewers, they learn to respect the creative efforts of others. The experience of envisioning and realizing a project together can lay the foundation for becoming effective workers and responsible community members once they leave school.

While movement and dance experiences emphasize individual expression, students are also constantly working with each other, either as fellow movers or collaborators.

```
D I A L O G U E
```

How can movement and dance help me teach my students?

_____

_____

What do I already know about working with movement and dance?

_____

_____

Who can I collaborate with in my school community? What
resources (artists, materials, references) are available to me?

_____

_____

How can I begin to use movement in my curriculum?

_____

_____

Authentic Expression

When I was twelve years old, I choreographed my first dance. My summer
dance teacher, Katherine Renouf, asked me to choreograph a dance and
perform it at a summer fair. Shortly after that, my aunt introduced me to
"Aysheh's Awakening" from the ballet *Spartacus,* and I fell in love with its
lush, romantic strains. Every day, for weeks, I hauled a record player with a
long extension cord out onto the lawn, and worked on the grass. My point
of departure was the idea of awakening. I began my dance on the ground
lying on my side. As the music murmured its beginning, my hand snaked its
way up towards the sky. Soon I was running, twirling, and leaping as the
music swelled more fully. At the end of the music, I returned to the reclining
shape in which I had begun. On the day of the performance, my concentration overcame any nervousness, and I communicated the "awakening" I had
discovered through dance.

Much later, in college, I trained seriously as a modern dancer. Developing
a strong and articulate instrument, learning about the craft of dance-
making—choreography—and seeing the work of great dance artists refined my creative abilities. But the seeds had been planted by Mrs. Renouf
and my dance teacher at school, Anita Zahn, who guided and encouraged
me to explore my responses to music and stories through movement. They

understood that dance is a natural way for children to express their exuberance and imaginative responses to life and the world around them.

As students move, they show what is in their hearts and minds. Their movements are authentic communication. The great modern dance pioneer, Martha Graham (1952) said it best: "There is a vitality, a life force, a quickening that is translated through you into action, and because there is only one of you in all time, this expression is unique." It is because we are unique that movement and dance works so well with children. Children can express their feelings, ideas, and points of view in individual ways and at their own level of ability and experience. Whether they are putting action words into motion, exploring the impact of gravity, or creating a dance about an ocean habitat, they will achieve a deeper understanding as they use movements to learn.

Chapter 2

What Is Movement and Dance?

D ance means different things to each of us. Our personal definition depends upon our own dance experiences and the dances we have seen. Depending on our cultural background, we may participate in a Native American ritual or dance the *hora* at a family wedding. Perhaps we've taken up square dancing as a means of socializing or African dance to understand more about our cultural heritage. Popular culture offers us, as viewers, everything from lively musical comedy numbers on stage, to the magic of Fred Astaire and Ginger Rogers on film, to the quickly-cutting images of dancers on television music videos.

What Is Dance?

Throughout time, dancing has been a way that people of all cultures experience and communicate what is meaningful to them. Human beings have danced to influence natural forces, to reinforce political and social orders, to pass on myths, to enact rituals, to enjoy themselves and each other, and to express themselves artistically.

Dance forms from around the globe like Spanish flamenco, Native American ceremonial dances, Japanese kabuki theater, European ballet, the capoeira of Brazil, African harvest dances, Indian classical dance, and American modern dance reflect the beliefs, values, and history of the cultures they spring from.

D I A L O G U E

What kind(s) of dance have I experienced as a mover? How were the experiences meaningful to me?

_____

_____

What kind(s) of dance have I experienced as a viewer? What was most meaningful to me about those viewing opportunities?

_____

_____

How would I characterize my relationship to dance? Dance is...

_____

_____

Dance is movement that transcends function and becomes communication.

Even though "dance" is a term that encompasses an extraordinarily diverse range of movement, perhaps the following definition which I have developed, can help us focus on its common features: *Dance is movement that transcends function and becomes communication. In order to communicate in this way, a dancer or group of dancers come together in an open space and perform crafted movements for an audience.*

Dance is a powerful form of communication because of the vital connection that exists between the dancers and the audience. The audience may be any

kind of observer—fellow students, community members, or paying patrons in a theater. Have you ever seen a dance performance that made you want to get up and dance? Or have you found yourself identifying with the feelings the dancers are expressing? Because human beings are innate, expressive movers, our muscles and spirits react sympathetically when we see dancers perform vibrant movement. It's as if each of us has a "moving self"—receiving and responding to the meaning of the dance.

S H O P T A L K

Jonas, Gerald. *Dancing: The Pleasure, Power, and Art of Movement.* New York: Harry N. Abrams in association with Thirteen/WNET, 1992.

Dancing is the companion volume of an eight-part series on dance that appeared on public television in 1993. The book is a succinct presentation of the material covered in the video series. Jonas has synthesized the contributuions of dance anthropologists, as well as dance artists, to describe and compare dance forms from around the globe. This well-written resource offers a historical and multicultural overview of dance that will deepen your knowledge of this diverse and dynamic field.

The Scope of *Dance as a Way of Knowing*

Dance as a Way of Knowing seeks to equip you with the tools to engage students as movers and creators as they learn about dance and make connections across the curriculum. To that end, this book offers strategies that come from a dance form known as *modern dance*.

Modern dance was created and has been sustained by artistic rebellion. In the early part of the twentieth century, Isadora Duncan (1877-1927) broke free from the restricted movements of ballet—a dance form that had originally developed in the courts of Europe. Where ballet sought to embody an idealized view of life, Duncan believed dance should express a human being's deepest responses to life. From her—and the work of modern dance pioneers like Martha Graham (1893-1991), Doris Humphrey (1895-1958), Hanya Holm (1898-1992), and Katherine Dunham (1909-)—sprang a tradition in which dancers rebelled against their artistic ancestors. An open-ended artistic process evolved that enabled dance artists to bring their individual visions to life.

When children are invited to work with movement strategies based on this open-ended process, they engage in a special kind of creative thinking. They make their own movement choices, and in turn, learn about dance. They are given the tools to communicate authentically and discover connections to other areas of their learning. They are not asked to imitate and perfect the movements of a particular dance form as performers.

This approach to movement and dance is akin to students' experiences with the visual arts. In art classes, they receive materials like paper, paint and brushes, as well as certain techniques for manipulating those materials effectively. With the teacher's help, they learn how to make their own artistic creations.

To understand the content and creative strategies of this approach, let's examine what a dance artist and painter have in common. The painter faces an empty canvas, and the dance artist confronts an empty space. The painter has brushes of various sizes, shapes, and thicknesses. The dancer has one instrument, the body, which can move in a variety of ways. A painter strokes different shapes, textures, and hues of paint onto a canvas. A dance artist creates movements of different shapes, speeds, and energies that unfold throughout the space. Both the painter and the dance artist put those choices together to make artistic wholes—a painting and a dance—which communicate the thoughts, feelings, or points of view of each artist.

The Elements of Dance

In order to create an expressive and meaningful dance, the dance artist (or choreographer) has to make decisions about the look, flow, and timing of the movements, drawing on the broad range of visual designs, qualities of motion, and rhythms that are possible in movement. These three areas known as *Space*, *Energy* (also called *Force* by some), and *Time* are the elements of dance. These elements help a dance artist discover movements which are expressive and unique. Just as a creative writer draws from a deep pool of words and phrases to communicate his or her ideas, so a dance artist needs a varied range of movements from which to choose.

- **Space** encompasses the overall design of movement—where it takes place in the space, as well as its size and shape.
- **Energy** involves the flow of motion—how movements are animated by kinetic energy in distinctive ways.
- **Time** includes how fast or slow movement is and whether it unfolds with its own natural rhythm, or is tied to a steady beat.

I'll describe the elements of dance in more detail in future chapters. For now, think of them as factors that make movement more defined and expressive. As modern dance pioneer Hanya Holm once said, "It's not *what* you do, it's *how* you do it, that's important."

Since our focus in movement and dance is to learn about the creative possibilities of movement rather than to perform specific dance steps, students engage in a process similar to that of the dance artist. They

- explore the expressive potential of the body
- become knowledgeable about the elements of dance
- learn how to select and sequence aesthetic movements.

Aesthetic Awareness

As you may already know, the term "aesthetic" refers to what we sense and feel when we behold something that has been carefully crafted—like a work of art. In the past, aesthetic has been associated with notions of beauty. Since what is considered beautiful can vary greatly among cultures and individuals, let's focus instead on the words "compelling" and "effective."

A dance is most effective when its movements inspire us to make meaning out of what we are witnessing.

Think of a memorable sunset you have seen. What was compelling about the experience? Perhaps your attention was drawn to uniquely shaped clouds streaked with gold and violet. As the sun dipped down, did the sky change from light blue to peach to deep red? Were gray shadows cast across the landscape? Just as vivid colors, shapes, and changes contribute to the impact and appeal of a sunset, so does the dance artist seek to infuse dance movements with distinctive shapes, contrasting energies, and surprising rhythms.

A dance is most effective when its movements inspire us to make meaning out of what we are witnessing. Think about what a sunset means to you. Some of us delight in how day transforms itself dramatically into night. For others, the encroaching shadows may sadly signal the passage of time.

Throughout this book, I'll highlight ways your students can develop their aesthetic awareness as movers, creators, and observers. Being conscious of ways to make movements compelling and effective will help students

- understand movement problems more deeply
- strengthen their knowledge of dance
- enable them to make more meaningful connections to other disciplines.

The Movement and Dance Learning Continuum

When I conduct movement and dance workshops, educators, understandably, have numerous questions about implementing movement strategies in their classrooms.

- How can we work in the classroom safely?
- How do we begin?
- How will my kids stay focused and not fly out of control?
- How can I structure and guide meaningful movement experiences?
- How can I help students integrate movement and dance across the curriculum?
- How do we assess our work in movement and dance?

To address the concerns and needs of classroom teachers, *Dance as a Way of Knowing* offers a progression of facilitation strategies which engages students in a three-phase learning continuum.

The Movement and Dance Learning Continuum

Natural —————————— Creative —————————— Artistic

Natural	Creative	Artistic
Students use existing movement.	Students develop discipline-based knowledge and creative problem-solving skills.	Students make dances and learn about dance as an art form.

The Natural Movement Phase
In the natural movement phase, students establish their spatial awareness and become responsible movers. They learn and show what they know through ordinary actions. It's an enjoyable and focusing way to begin working with movement in the classroom. Here are a few examples of how your students can work with natural movement. They can

- create gestures while singing a song
- move as quietly as possible from one work area to another
- explore movements associated with work
- put verbs, adverbs, and prepositions into action.

The Creative Movement Phase

The creative movement phase is the heart of the movement and dance process. Students focus on the process of exploration and creative problem solving as they

- learn about the dance elements of Space, Energy, and Time
- move beyond the limits of natural movement and make in-depth connections across the curriculum
- create short movement sequences and group studies.

The Artistic Movement Phase

Sylvia Ashton Warner (1995) describes her experience with dance in her classroom. "It just happened one bright spring morning when I was playing some Schubert to please no one but myself, that a child stood up from his work and began composing a dance, then another and another, and there it all was, and here it all is."

In the artistic movement phase, students

- focus on making dances
- relate their efforts to the work of various dance artists, either through live performances or videos, to deepen their understanding of the discipline.

Field Notes: Teacher-To-Teacher

At the conclusion of Project Endangered, where science, mathematics, and language arts became integrated around the theme of endangerment, every group in our combined sixth-grade classes presented their interpretation of the destruction of the rain forest and the extinction of animal species through music and dance. The selection of music, the sounds of the rain forest, student choreography, make-up, and costuming truly brought an increased depth of understanding and feelings of human emotion to each group's area of worldwide research.

Char Girard and Richard Jacobsen
Emma W. Shuey Elementary School
Rosemead, California

SHOPTALK

Consortium of National Arts Education Associations. *National Standards for Arts Education.* Reston, Virginia: Music Educators National Conference, 1994.

The national standards were developed by the Consortium of National Arts Education Associations to determine what every young American should know and be able to do in dance.

The standards students are expected to achieve include

- understanding dance as a way to create and communicate meaning
- making connections between dance and healthful living
- identifying and demonstrating movement elements and skills in performing dance
- understanding choreographic principles, processes, and structures
- applying and demonstrating critical and creative thinking skills
- making connections between dance and other disciplines
- demonstrating and understanding dance in various cultures and historical periods.

The standards exist to encourage the teaching of dance with integrity in schools across the nation and to provide students with sound, high-level experiences in dance. Overall, the movement and dance strategies I discuss support the fulfillment of the content and achievement standards proposed in the dance portion of the *National Standards for Arts Education.*

How To Use This Book

Even though this book is designed to meet the concerns and realities of K-6 classroom teachers, your instructional goals, prior knowledge, and individual learning styles vary. Some of you may be starting your investigation of movement and dance and may feel most comfortable following a clear-cut, step-by-step progression of facilitation strategies. If you have a background in dance and are looking to integrate movement into your instruction, you may choose to jump into the creative movement phase. Others may want their students to observe dance before involving them in creative strategies. Whatever your goals, interests, and needs, here's how the chapters relate to the movement and dance learning continuum:

Chapter 3, Getting into Action, helps you become more aware of what you already know about movement. It focuses on beginning facilitation strategies as you guide your students to connect their natural movements to their learning in other disciplines.

Chapters 4, 5, and 6 constitute the creative movement phase and employ increasingly sophisticated strategies to maximize your students' concentration, creativity, and collaboration skills. Chapters 4 and 5, Moving into Understanding and Moving into Exploration and Discovery, focus on the elements of dance and increasingly rich curriculum connections. Chapter 6, How To Design Your Own Lessons, walks you through the "Movement and Dance Lesson Framework" so you can create your own lessons.

Chapter 7, Moving into Artistic Expression, focuses on the artistic movement phase. It offers guiding questions for looking at dance, resources for deepening your knowledge about dance, and guidelines for helping your students make and present their own dances.

Collaborating with colleagues. The first plunge into working with movement and dance can be made easier if you team up to plan and share facilitation responsibilities. Share practical information and support each other as you try new strategies.

DIALOGUE

What are my strengths as a teacher?

_____

_____

Based on what I know so far, how will these strengths help me facilitate movement and dance experiences?

_____

_____

Who can I work with on my staff to integrate movement and dance into the curriculum?

_____

_____

Accessing Your Expertise

Let's acknowledge the expertise you may already bring to facilitating movement experiences.

- Communication skills are essential for guiding movement experiences.

- Sensitivity to the attention and energy levels of your whole class, as well as individual students, helps you decide how and when to focus on movement.

- Understanding your students' developmental maturity helps you identify the best curriculum concepts to use, as well as how to structure a progression of lessons over a period of time.

- Creativity—to see and meet a need in an inventive fashion—helps you design your own movement lessons.

- Assessing whether an activity is working, and spontaneously changing course to go in a more productive direction, can help you build your expertise as a facilitator of movement and dance.

- Willingness to take risks will allow students to develop and strengthen their creativity as they investigate their own movement choices.

You've just identified many of the skills that will help you guide movement lessons. In the next chapter, you'll discover and build on motion you experience every day of your life.

Chapter 3

Getting into Action

Trust only movement. Life happens at the level of events, not of words. Trust movement.

Alfred Adler

One of my workshops' culminating activities focused on using movement and dance as a tool for learning in the classroom. During this activity, participants created and demonstrated model learning events. Teachers discovered how to make exciting connections between movement and curriculum areas. When I invited everyone to share what they had learned in their collaborative groups, one educator said, "Nothing came together until we got up and moved."

Her response inspired a flurry of nods from her colleagues. Most had started the workshop with some trepidation, since moving in open-ended and expressive ways was such a new experience for them. But in the end, they understood the importance of "getting into motion" to learn.

In this chapter, you'll explore what you already know about a broad spectrum of movement. Then I'll invite you to get into action with some clear-cut and effective strategies. I will strive to show you that

- learning about movement and dance is a highly focused and structured experience which builds logically on what we already know about movement

- facilitation is primarily verbal and does not depend on a teacher's skills as a mover
- students can explore movement ideas in existing classroom space.

Exploring Natural Movement

Working with natural movement is the easiest way for you and your students to start, and it will help you develop a strong foundation for future learning experiences. How do you learn about natural movement? Start by gathering information from your kinesthetic sense.

The kinesthetic sense. Just as we rely on our senses of taste, touch, smell, hearing, and vision to function, so do the sensory experiences of movement help us make our way through life. We use our kinesthetic sense to receive and act on information as we move. While walking down a flight of stairs we may see where the next step is, but our kinesthetic sense tells us how it feels to place our weight on that step. As we continue down the stairs, this sense tells our body what it needs to do—bend our knees, swing our arms from side to side, touch the railing with our hand—to maintain our balance. It all happens so quickly and naturally that we are barely conscious of our reliance on our kinesthetic sense.

Just as we rely on our senses of taste, touch, smell, hearing, and vision to function, so do the sensory experiences of movement help us make our way through life.

To become more aware of your kinesthetic sense, take a moment to feel, not look at, the position you are sitting in. Is your spine straight or slumped? Where are your arms? Are you legs bent or straight? Are your feet touching the ground? Are your shoulders hunched or relaxed? Your kinesthetic sense is giving you all the answers.

Tune in to all the movements you use as you go about your day. How do you sit, stand, lift, lower, twist, turn, and lie down? While walking, become aware of how different parts of the body move. Your arms probably *swing* back and forth while your knees *bend* and *lift,* permitting your heels to transfer your weight onto the ground. Feel the difference between a slow stroll and a frantic rush.

If you exercise regularly, or participate in sports, tune into the muscular sensations of running, throwing and catching a ball, lifting weights, stretching, or swimming. Even though the whole body is moving, what specific body parts and what energies do you highlight as you perform those actions? For instance, in swimming, we usually *stroke smoothly* with our arms, and *kick vigorously* with our legs to propel ourselves through water.

Remember—you don't have to be a dancer to be an effective facilitator. But, it does help to be on friendly terms with your potential as a moving, expressive human being. Often it's not our lack of desire or knowledge that prevents us from working with movement in the classroom, but a negative attitude toward ourselves as movers.

Let's step back a moment into our childhood. Chances are we were once natural, exuberant movers—just as our students are today. Gradually, social pressure and maturation taught us to control our actions. Unfortunately, as adults, we may now hardly move at all. Think about it. If we let go and dance out of pure joy at a social function, friends may call us a *ham*. Nevertheless, we shouldn't feel inhibited about expressing ourselves through movement. After all, our urge to move is inherently human and may inspire others to express their vitality, too.

If you are not currently involved in some kind of regular physical activity, think about walking around your neighborhood more often, attending a class for adult beginners in tap dancing, tai chi, yoga, or modern dance, or joining a country dance group in your community. Not only will it enhance your physical well-being, it will help you access more possibilities when working with your students.

Different ways of seeing. It's also possible to build your movement knowledge through observation. You might ask, where do I begin to look? The entire universe is filled with motion, but look in particular at the following movement laboratories:

- nature
- your town square
- sporting events
- your very own classroom.

Nature offers a varied and stimulating spectrum of movement. Think of clouds that *drift* across the sky; birds that *soar, dive,* and *hop;* a river that *cascades* down a mountainside. To enhance your movement awareness, try this. Look at a garden, a tree, a clump of woods, a balcony with a few plants, a pond—any setting outside where squirrels might be darting about, or dragonflies hovering. Give yourself time to concentrate. Record your observations as specifically as possible. Is the wind making the leaves sway or shiver? Becoming more sensitive to distinctions in movement will help you build the visual and verbal tools with which to guide movement explorations.

Dance specialist Patty Yancey shared with me kindergartner William Freeland's observation, "Wind is exercise for the trees." Ask your students to write down movements they observe in nature. Finding descriptors and images that capture specific motions, as William did, will strengthen their oral and written skills.

People-watching in town or city centers, at a county fair, or even at the local shopping mall, is a rewarding and easy way to do movement research. Observe the natural actions of passersby. Are they communicating something about who they are by the way they walk, stand, or look around? If so, what and how? What kinds of gestures do they use while talking? Are they losing patience, thrilled to see a friend, or feeling vulnerable and alone? Keep a running list of powerful action words and movement descriptors for expressive, nonverbal movement such as *dash* or *slouch, stride purposefully,* or *explode with laughter.*

Rather than focusing on the competitive aspects of a sporting event, try to identify the movements the players are using. For example, basketball often looks like a high-powered dance as players pair up and move in short, jagged steps throughout the space. One player, the soloist, runs down the court with large, graceful leaps while bouncing a ball. He twists, turns, then jumps with tremendous force into the air, and stays suspended long enough to stuff the ball into the basket.

Assessing the Needs and Abilities of Your Students

Nowhere is it more valuable to tune into the innate, unique expressiveness of human movement than in your classroom. The more conversant you are with the ways your students can and like to move, the more you will be able to make constructive choices about how and when to work with movement.

Start paying attention to your students' natural movements and body language. How do they move? Try distinguishing the differences between their *locomotor* steps—jumping, hopping, skipping, galloping, and sliding. What kinds of movements tell you they are keyed up? tired? focused? What are their strengths and weaknesses in terms of spatial awareness and self-control?

As you develop a "movement profile" of your class, you'll become aware of students'

individual movement styles. Who pirouettes to the locker and back? Who throws slow-motion baseballs in between science lessons? Who sits quietly most of the day? You will probably identify several kinesthetic learners who can readily use movement to show you what they know.

As you understand students' movement styles, you'll increasingly know how to guide individuals in group experiences. If students are usually shy about moving, but allow themselves to participate more fully, you'll be able to register and acknowledge their progress even though their movements may not be as expansive as those of others. And you can challenge excited, inventive movers who unwittingly intrude on the space of others to channel their energy. There's no need to admonish them for their exuberance.

How To Guide Natural Movement Experiences

As a learner you've been asked to sense, observe, describe, and explore movement that exists within you and surrounds you. Now, it's time to focus on how to facilitate movement experiences with your students.

As you develop a "movement profile" of your class, you'll be able to make choices about how to work with movement.

Special Moments in Your Classroom

One of the simplest ways to get started is to infuse movement into special moments that already exist in your classroom throughout the day.

Celebrations. How can movements take the place of words in greeting and leave-taking activities, or birthday and holiday celebrations? Use movements to accompany a good morning song, or other song that reinforces a sense of community within your classroom. You can use gestures that express the literal meaning of words, reflect the rhythm, or simply capture the feelings the song is expressing.

The Name Game. One activity you might consider is the Name Game. It's a follow-the-leader activity that's easy for everyone to learn. Start by inviting your class to stand in a circle. Tell everyone you'd like them to echo how you say your name and the gesture you make. Model this strategy yourself to help get the ball rolling. Make a simple gesture—like snapping your fingers—and say your name at the same time. Then ask everyone in the circle to echo your name and gesture. Try it again, this time with a different gesture. Then ask a child next to you to try it, and proceed once around the circle. For the second go-around, ask everyone to say their name and make a gesture that communicates something they'd like everyone to know about them. You'll see a variety of movements. Some children may exhibit a flash of their personalities, some may share moves from a favorite sport or hobby.

Ask students what they learned about their classmates from watching and echoing their movements. Then ask for descriptions of the kinds of movements students used to communicate information about themselves.

Sharpening their powers of observation will reinforce what they are learning as movers.

Transitions. If your students sit for a long time and then get up and move to another area or part of the school, you can make those transitions more focused or purposeful. Have them show you how *quietly* they can *rise up* from their chairs and get into line. As students move on to another activity, you can also ask them to demonstrate through movement the characteristics of people they've just been learning about in literature or social studies.

Stillness. Do your students ever have a chance to be completely still or relaxed? Even though our emphasis in movement and dance is on motion, stillness is also an important part of the experience. There are two kinds of stillness we use in dance—active stillness, a highly energized form of halted motion, and passive stillness, in which all the muscles give into gravity and relax. Resting their heads and arms on their desks, while experiencing absolute passive stillness, allows students to wind down and refocus their energies.

How To Work with Movement in the Classroom

Before you use full-bodied movement as a tool for learning, both you and your students need to learn how to work with movement in the classroom. This crucial step is often overlooked, and unfortunately, disregarding it can lead to unsuccessful rather than productive experiences. Before you plunge into action you'll need to

- access what your students already know about movement
- develop your students' listening skills
- help your students identify where they are and focus themselves in the space they occupy.

Exploring what students already know about movement. I often begin a movement and dance experience by asking, "What kinds of movement do we do because we are human beings?"

One intrepid soul usually offers an answer which is soon followed by a cascade of responses.

"Talk," "Breathe," "Walk," "Run," "Jump," "Stretch," "Throw." Generating a list of actions will focus your students on the task at hand, help them articulate what they already know, and access their built-in movement vocabulary. Try to refer to the words on the list as you guide your students' movement experiences.

Ground rules for working with movement. Next, I ask students what agreements they can make with me and each other to ensure everyone has a positive experience while working with movement. Their list might include

- don't bump
- watch where you're going
- don't talk
- listen for directions.

Focusing students on listening. In many ways a movement lesson is a multi-sensory experience. While students focus on moving, they are guided by listening to verbal directions that suggest how to move, and prompts from a drum that both cue and stop their movements. As you observe them respond to your directions, you'll discover what they should concentrate on or do next.

To get started, it's helpful to test students' listening skills with simple commands and drum cues while they are still sitting in their chairs. Since they are not up and moving yet, this allows you to give directions, cue movements, and watch within clear limits. It challenges your students to focus on following the commands and translating them into action.

"Commands" are succinct, clear, verbal directions that are shared over the course of a movement lesson to ensure comprehension without interfering in the overall flow of the movement experience. Lengthy directions can overwhelm students. Long explanations load on too many tasks, and can drain the life blood out of a lesson by focusing on words rather than movement.

Here is an example of effective directions:

> "When I hit the drum, raise your hands to the ceiling."
>
> A strike of the drum.
>
> Students lift their arms over their heads and hold them there. Their eyes gleam

with satisfaction. You just gave them a direction they could follow easily and immediately.

> "When I hit the drum, lower your arms as slowly as you can."
>
> A strike of the drum.
>
> Students lower their arms, engrossed by this simple task. No one has ever asked them to move this way before. They make their own choices, but within the limits of *lower* and *slowly*. If they look around, they'll notice everyone has different ways to "lower your arms as slowly as you can."

Brief commands engage students' *kinesthetic intelligences* right away. They do not need everything explained before they move. Students need to think and learn through moving.

How to start and stop movement. The drum is a great facilitation tool. Waiting for a drum beat to cue movement gives students time to absorb the verbal directions you've just given them and promotes a positive sense of expectancy, because they are eager to translate the words they have just heard into their very own actions.

A strong whack of the drum can also be used to tell students when to *freeze* their actions on the spot. Students are now primed to listen to the next set of directions, cued by another strike of the drum. Pausing in active stillness keeps their attention and energy alive.

Freeze. Students delight in the challenge of moving—then stopping on a dime. As any student of physics knows, to stop the natural momentum of an object in motion, especially the body, requires energy.

Try this. As you shake your hands out in front of you fairly vigorously, ask a family member or friend to clap sharply when you least expect it...whap! Now freeze your hands as quickly as you can. You may notice that your hands jiggle for a second after you hear the clap, even though you stopped shaking them. Absolute arrested motion does not result just from stopping what you're doing; you have to actively tense your muscles, too. To understand the difference, repeat the shake-stop sequence. This time when you hear the clap, freeze your hands into fists, claws, and then fully extend your fingers. Feel the difference? See the difference?

Try this with your students to help them understand the criteria for freezing into active stillness. The key factors—being in motion, listening for the cue to stop, using energy in order to freeze quickly and strongly— can be transposed from their hands to the larger challenges of moving with their whole bodies.

Other sound sources. You can cue and stop movement using a variety of percussion instruments like wooden blocks or triangles. Tap on an empty coffee can with a plastic lid or a table-top with a ruler. In the beginning, it's helpful to stop movement by giving a sharp "whap!" with whatever you use, so students can echo the sound with their movement. Later, when students have become more adept at controlling their movements, you can use visual signals, like flashing the lights off and on, or, if all eyes can be upon you safely and easily, special movements of your own devising.

Spatial Awareness

Besides listening to directions, the next most important area for students to concentrate on is space—both the area they are working in, called the *workspace*, and the area each individual is moving in, called *personal space*.

The workspace. Before you involve your students in a movement experience, you need to decide where they'll work. A large, open space like a multi-purpose room gives students plenty of space in which to move, but most learning events can be implemented in your classroom.

In your classroom, you have several options. Students can move in "available space" through the aisles between desks and tables. Upcoming lessons model how to divide the class into alternating groups to avoid traffic problems. To create more space for your students, move tables, desks, and chairs to the periphery of your classroom. You can guide third- through sixth-grade students to clear the furniture and replace it when the movement lesson is finished. Another choice is to have small groups of students demonstrate their work in an open space near the front of the room, while the rest of the class observes.

Working in a multi-purpose room or gymnasium allows the whole class to move all at once or break into smaller groups. If you're in an extremely large gymnasium, use the lines painted on the floor to establish the parameters of the workspace, so students can see and hear you.

Personal space. The next learning events are designed to develop students' awareness of their personal space. Learning how to move in one place and through space, while being sensitive to the personal space of others, will enable students to engage in all subsequent learning events successfully. You'll notice that all learning events end with reflection.

Be sure to

- read through the whole lesson to get a sense of the progression
- visualize your students following each set of directions as you read through the learning event
- think of what you need to say and do to prompt their movements
- internalize an outline of the steps, or post the outline on a nearby wall in big lettering to help you stay on track (see the "Lesson Outline" on page 40)
- gather materials you'll need, like a drum.

An important area for students to concentrate on is space—both the area they are working in, called the workspace, *and the area each individual is moving in, called* personal space.

Learning Event

Spatial Awareness—In Place

Introduction. Focus students on the purpose of this first movement lesson by linking it to your students' discussion of ground rules. Guide them to understand that each student needs to learn how to be a responsible, considerate mover so that everyone can have a positive and productive movement experience.

To begin. Invite the whole class to stand up and move their chairs under their desks as quietly as they can at the sound of the drum. Notice how this small act of concentration focuses your students' attention and reduces the noise level in your room.

Establishing a home base. Ask everyone to observe all the empty spaces in the classroom—next to their tables, desks or learning centers, in the aisles, in the front, back, and sides of the room. Explain that you are going to ask everyone to find a spot on which they can move without bumping into anything or anyone.

Ask three to five student volunteers to model what everyone else will be doing. At the sound of the drum, have each member of this small group walk to a spot which is not too close to the furniture, walls, or anyone else. Have each student label this spot his or her home base.

To promote "ownership" of their home bases, ask these students to perform a four-action sequence cued by single drum beats:

"Raise your arms to the ceiling."

A strike of the drum. Students comply.

"Reach your arms out to the side."

A strike of the drum. Students comply.

"Turn all the way around."

A strike of the drum. Students comply.

"Clap your hands and freeze."

A strike of the drum. Students comply.

Ask the next group of students to find spots they can stand on. Each time a new group finds their home bases, have everyone repeat the ownership sequence together. Repeat finding home base until all students have found a spot.

Movement exploration. Once all the students have filled the workspace and are at least an arm's length away from each other, the walls, and the furniture, have them focus on the area that surrounds them. This area is called their *personal space*.

Depending on their age and interests, students can imagine they are in a "bubble" (primary) or "spaceship" (upper). I've found it helpful to blow real soap bubbles for younger students so they can see the shape and transparency of bubbles. This way, they can also see how easily bubbles pop.

Give students time to establish the inside parameters of their bubble or spaceship by asking them to

- reach their whole bodies up as high as they can

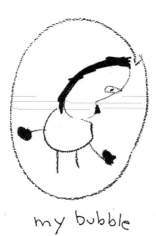

my bubble

- reach as low as they can without sitting down
- reach to the side from low to high, tracing the sides of their bubble or spaceships
- reach their whole bodies forward and back without moving off their home bases.

Give them eight drum beats to move inside of their personal space any way they want. (The drumbeats provide the amount of time for them to move. Students are not expected to move in sync with each beat.) Encourage them to find movements that are their very own, and like no one else's. Ask them to freeze the shape they find themselves in at the end of eight drum beats.

Repeat this at least three times—asking them to find different ways to explore the inside of their bubble or spaceship each time. They should be moving very freely within the limits of their bubble or spaceship.

Reflection. Have students return to their seats and ask them to describe the different kinds of movements they experienced while exploring their personal space. With their responses, you can build a class "movement vocabulary" by posting it in the classroom and adding to it after each movement experience. Students can draw upon the list to write about their movement experiences and you can use key words or images to guide future movement experiences. Ten-year-old Devora Kaye describes exploring her personal space:

Enclosing, Flexing, Wiggling, Shaking, Reaching.

You can post this sample outline of the steps to help you facilitate the spatial awareness learning event.

Lesson Outline

1. Students stand up and observe empty spaces.
2. Small group finds home base.
3. Students perform ownership sequence when they arrive:
    - raise up arms
    - reach to the side
    - turn around
    - clap/freeze.
4. Other groups find home base and perform sequence.
5. Students establish "bubble" or "spaceship."
6. They have eight drum beats to move inside personal space and freeze last shape. Repeat three times.
7. List movements.

Field Notes: Teacher-To-Teacher

Individuals and cultures in general have very different concepts of acceptable "personal space." Exercises that help students develop sensitivity to others' need for space will reduce tension in the classroom, generally caused by close quarters. One useful activity is to encourage students to find the maximum distance between themselves in a particular space (classroom, gymnasium). This means filling up the area with evenly-spaced students. Then, ask students to move around slowly, still trying to keep the maximum distance. Give oral instructions for students to speed up or slow down, and mention areas of the room which are congested so students can adjust. Occasionally, ask students to congregate all together at a particular spot to demonstrate minimum personal space, and then spread out again. This activity ties in nicely with the study of urban and rural environments.

Gregory Acker
Artist Educator
Louisville, Kentucky

Traveling through Space

Taking responsibility for their personal space enables students to work effectively with others in the workspace. So far, they have concentrated on motion that occurs in place (also known as *axial movement*). Now they are ready to travel through space (also known as *locomotor movement*). Whether moving in place or traveling through space, students are expected to stay within the confines of their personal space and avoid popping someone else's bubble or crashing into someone else's spaceship.

Learning Event

Spatial Awareness—Through Space

Introduction. Invite students to meet challenges of moving clearly and responsibly through the space.

To begin. Have students stand on their home bases and revisit the limits of their personal space. Have them look around so they know exactly where their home bases are located. Ask them count off into 1s and 2s. Explain that you are going to ask 1s to walk away and return to their home bases in sixteen drum beats. For primary grades, begin with eight drum beats. Before they move, play the drum at a moderate speed and count along, so they hear how much time they have to complete the task.

Movement exploration. Challenge 1s to walk, watch where they are going, and maintain the integrity of their personal space. Challenge 2s to freeze in a small shape either sitting or standing on their home bases while 1s travel through the space. (If the workspace is particularly cramped, you might try dividing your class into three or four groups.)

With your drum, cue 1s to travel and 2s to freeze, counting the drum beats aloud as you play them. Then give 2s the chance to travel, while 1s freeze on their home bases. Repeat this activity several times.

Students reflect on their movement experiences to connect to their learning in individual ways.

Because this activity not only asks them to travel—it also asks them to plan—don't be surprised if you hear excited exclamations or giggles if they miscalculate how far off their home bases they can go and get back to by the last drum beat. It's a good idea to acknowledge this new experience and then resume the lesson. Your students will need to repeat this whole activity at least two or three times before they can master it.

Their next challenge will be to travel in ways other than walking. Remind them to focus on moving clearly and responsibly through the space. To elicit different traveling steps, ask them to change *how* they are going off and back to their home base.

Reflection. Once students have returned to their seats, ask them to describe what they just did. Be prepared for a variety of responses. Some will report the kinds of movements they were engaged in, the images that arose in their minds while moving, or how they met the goals of not bumping into each other and getting back to their home base in time. Next, ask students how the whole experience *felt*. Remember to validate their responses. You may want to jot down some notes from your discussion in your class movement profile.

Learning to maintain personal space doesn't happen with the first experience. Students will have to engage in this experience several times. Ask students to be conscious of their personal space during other times at school, such as when they are traveling from your classroom to another part of the school, and at home when they're sharing space with their families. Eventually, maintaining personal space will become second nature. Once students establish their spatial awareness, it will enable them to focus fully on the content of exciting movement tasks.

You've just employed strategies that are central to *all* movement and dance lessons. Before we explore how your students can use natural movement to deepen their understanding of various curriculum topics, take a moment to review what you've learned so far about facilitating movement experiences.

DIALOGUE

How can my students show what they already know about movement?

_____

_____

How can I inspire my students to move freely yet within clearly defined limits?

_____

_____

How can I cue and stop their movements? establish the length of movements?

_____

_____

How can I help them maintain their focus and self-control?

_____

_____

How can I challenge them to build on what they already know?

_____

_____

How can my students reflect on their experience?

_____

_____

How To Make Curriculum Connections

You don't understand anything until you learn it more than one way.

Marvin Minsky

Now that your students know how to focus their energy, respond to simple directions, and move responsibly in the space, they are ready to explore curriculum connections with concentration and freedom. They will reinforce, develop, or extend knowledge in other disciplines and show what they know about a curriculum area through movement.

Aesthetic Awareness

In all movement and dance experiences, you are asking students to be *mindful* as they move, to fill their minds and actions with the intention of moving in specific ways. The movements students discover and perform then, no matter how ordinary, can be defined and effective.

In all movement and dance experiences, you are asking students to be mindful *as they move, to fill their minds and actions with the intention of moving in specific ways.*

Keep an eye out for movement that is indicated and not enacted in a full-bodied way. Indicated movement is the kinesthetic equivalent of shorthand. If, for example, a child is simulating the act of chopping down a tree only with her hands, she is not discovering movement that is full-bodied and specific. Also, be aware of whether students are moving clearly or not (the kinesthetic equivalent of mumbling). If students' motions are rushed or blurred, I often make an analogy to speaking. I intentionally mumble some words and ask if they can understand me. Then I enunciate the words more clearly and ask them to enact their movements with equal clarity. As always, encourage all students, especially in the beginning, to find their own movements. Challenge them to discover movements that are "unlike anyone else's."

Reflective journals. Students can keep track of what they're learning in a movement and dance journal. You might ask them to record what they learned about working with movement, what they learned about the curriculum topic or theme, and what they'd like to learn about next. Be sure to give students the opportunity to share their responses with you and each other.

You can jot down ideas for future movement and dance projects and curriculum connections in your movement and dance journal. Your journal can also serve as a place to keep anecdotal notes on students' interests and progress. I find that keeping a journal is a helpful assessment tool.

What follows is a description of the ways you can guide students to explore topics in social studies, math, and language arts through natural movement. These strategies serve as models that you will no doubt take from and add to as you become more experienced in working with movement.

Social Studies Connection

Students learn in social studies that all people perform tasks to maintain their survival. We call these actions "work." Household chores enacted by caring adults and children, the labor of neighborhood workers, and the actions of colonial farmers all lend themselves to meaningful exploration through movement.

...If You Lived in Colonial Times by Ann McGovern, illustrated by June Otani, is full of information about the life and work of this country's early settlers. Some tasks from those times include chopping down trees, hauling logs, and crafting planks of wood. To understand how physically challenging life was in colonial times, students can get up and explore work actions through full-bodied motion.

Movement exploration. Ask students to list and distinguish work actions which occur in place and through space. Have students move out onto their home bases and establish the parameters of their personal space. Ask everyone to explore a work activity that occurs in place. You can choose an action for primary grades, while older children can select their own actions from the list they've created.

Guide primary students by calling out an action a certain number of times, such as "chop, chop, chop, chop." Prompt older students to explore an action sequence. For example, they can pick up an ax, chop away, and fell a tree in eight drum beats.

Have students count off into 1s and 2s. Then ask them, in alternating groups, to explore an action or action sequence that travels off and back to home base in sixteen drum beats. Invite students to explore a third action that takes place on their home base.

Culminating sequence. To consolidate their learning, guide students to put the three work activities together into a sequence. You can select a sequence for primary grades, and upper elementary students may choose their own.

Primary
- chop 4 times
- travel off then back to home base hauling a heavy log for 16 drum beats
- saw 4 times

Upper
- chop for 8 drum beats
- travel off then back to home base hauling a heavy log for 16 drum beats
- saw, plane, sand for 16 drum beats

Encourage students to find unique ways to enact these tasks. Have them repeat the sequence several times, so their actions can flow from one to the other without stopping. This way, students can transform their understanding of work actions into movement expression.

Field Notes: Teacher-To-Teacher

Children can get up and have a quick but memorable learning experience right next to their desks. My third graders explore the meaning of some difficult word concepts by acting them out. For example, students visualize they are hawks and use arm and body movements to understand the word "swooping."

Mary Tappan
Mildred B. Janson School
Rosemead, California

Math Connection

Fifth-grade teacher Laura Gray, of the Billy Mitchell School in Lawndale, California, devised a sign language for math computation which I saw her use to focus her class after recess. Gray stood in front of her class and flashed her fingers in different combinations. Then she made straight-lined shapes with her forearms. After a few seconds of watching her move, I realized she was engaging her class in a series of addition, subtraction, and multiplication computations. Her fingers were signifying numbers and her forearms were creating symbols: a vertical and horizontal cross shape with her arms signified addition; a horizontal line with her forearm indicated a minus sign; her forearms crossed in an "x" shape represented the multiplication sign; a parallel shape with both lower arms stood for the equal sign. She engaged her class in a lengthy string of silent computations, and then invited a student to come up to the front of the room and lead the class.

This strategy could be adapted as a math connection for lower grades as they learn basic computations. Once you have modeled it for the entire class, students can work together in small groups.

Extension. Invite students to research, demonstrate, and compare different forms of nonverbal communication such as

- universal expressive gestures
- American Sign Language

- Native American Sign Language
- gestures of musical conductors, traffic officers, and sports referees.

The following learning event is designed to enhance students' awareness of spatial relationships as well as their language comprehension. Instead of verbalizing the directions, you might try writing them on the chalkboard and asking your students to follow them. As the learning event progresses, students are asked to create a sequence of expressive movements which demonstrates their understanding of action words and relationships in space.

Learning Event

Spatial Relationships and Language

Introduction. Focus students on the purpose of this lesson.

To begin. Ask your students to move their chairs far enough away from their desks and into available space so that they can stand up, sit down, and move around their chairs freely.

Movement exploration. Explain that you are going to call out (or point to) a series of commands you want students to put into motion so they can explore their relationship to objects and people in the space.

Command sequence:

"Stand up."

"Skip around your chair."

"Wave your arms high above your chair."

"Touch the back of your seat with one hand, and stretch the rest of your body as far from your chair as you can."

"Take three hops away from your chair and freeze."

"After you sway your body two times, go stand as near as you can to someone else without touching."

"Before sliding back to your chair, creep over to the nearest wall and freeze for three seconds." (They can look at their watches or the wall clock.)

"Sit down."

Creative problem solving. Go through each command as many times as it takes for everyone to understand the actions and spatial relationships. Ask students to enact each set of directions accurately, without stopping. For example, insist they execute *three hops away* from their chair and *freeze immediately* into a shape of their choice. Each verbal command, in turn, inspires a "movement phrase."

Aesthetic awareness. Built into each command is an invitation to find their own way to carry out a set of actions. Students enjoy solving these movement problems, especially when they can invest the solutions with their own energy and choices. Encourage them to find inventive ways to stand, skip, wave, stretch, hop, freeze, sway, slide, creep, and sit.

Once students are comfortable working with movement, they can reinforce what they're learning by viewing each other's efforts.

Here's a tip. If their traveling steps are noisy, challenge students to skip, hop, and slide as *quietly* as they can. This will help them lift their weight—not clunk it into the ground—which will sharpen their physical skills.

Culminating sequence. Choose or ask students to select two to four of the directions to put together. For instance, students can connect three commands into one sequence and perform it without stopping: "Stand up, skip around your chair, and sit down." Once students grasp the task, you can challenge them to keep adding to their sequences. Upper elementary students will be able to internalize the entire list of directions to create one long sequence.

As always, students need time and practice to put sequences together. Since they'll be up and moving in the classroom, remind them to exercise strong spatial awareness so everyone can work comfortably. If your classroom is too cramped, have half or one third of the class work on the sequence at a time.

Music. Consider playing selections of New Age music with an underlying beat, such as Enya's *Shepherd Moon,* to accompany students as they put their sequences into motion. Then invite five students at a time to demonstrate their sequences as seamlessly as possible.

Observation. Once students are comfortable working with movement, they can reinforce what they're learning by viewing each other's efforts. They're able to see what they are doing by observing how their classmates fulfill the same movement problems. It is critical, however, to set up viewing guidelines so that everyone shows their work in a safe, respectful environment. Start by sharing with your students the purpose of viewing each other's work. Stress that observation is a visual tool to help them deepen their learning in movement and dance.

Viewing guidelines. Ask students to generate ground rules for observing each other's work. Ground rules inspire considerate attitudes towards their classmates and will help students be good audience members when they see any kind of performance.

Ground rules might include

- respect everyone's work
- no comments while others are moving
- pay attention to those who are showing their work.

It's also helpful to focus students on what they will be looking for as they share their work with each other. Devise questions that recall the movement task they are fulfilling like, "What is each group supposed to do? What kinds of movement is everyone supposed to be working with?"

After students share their work, solicit general responses to what they just witnessed by asking, "What did you see?" Remember, students will tune in and respond in different ways.

Then guide them to analyze what they just saw by asking them to

- label the different kinds of movement they observed
- describe how and where their classmates traveled in the space.

At this point, you just want to get their powers of observation and articulation about movement going. In later chapters, I discuss establishing criteria and guidelines for helping your students evaluate what they are seeing.

Reflection. Ask students to write in their movement and dance journals about their work process. How did they put the commands into action? construct their movement sequences? Where and how did they move in the classroom? What might they change about what they did? Why? Encourage them also to describe any observations or associations they had while moving around their chairs and through the space.

Assessment. As you work with movement and dance, your eye will become more adept at assessing the varying skill levels of your students as participants, movers, explorers, and communicators. At this point, I recommend two types of evaluation:

- continuous assessment which occurs while you are guiding movement experiences
- assessment of the sequences you ask them to put together and perform.

Portrait of a Concentrated, Skilled Natural Mover

One way to develop the standards and expectations to assess your students' work is to create a portrait of a student working at the highest possible level in the natural movement phase. Here is a sample portrait of a middle elementary student, followed by variations for younger and older children.

Participation. The student listens, follows directions accurately, and is always alert to the next set of directions; is sensitive to personal space and the space and efforts of others; is able to access and build on prior knowledge; and can apply what has been learned in previous movement explorations to new learning experiences.

Movement. The student understands the difference between *axial* (in place) and *locomotor* (through space) movement. The student is able to distinguish between different locomotor forms, to explore the same movement task in different ways, and to connect "movement phrases" into a sequence.

Aesthetic awareness. *As a mover:* The student moves in full-bodied and specific ways with concentration, energy, and clarity; generates original movements; and is able to perform sequences with a sense of flow. *As an observer:* The student is able to label different kinds of natural movements, and to describe the differences between movements and how movements are meaningful to him or her.

Curriculum content. The student is able to demonstrate knowledge of a specific curriculum concept—like action words and spatial relationships—through accurate, detailed movements and sequences of movement. The student can reflect upon and articulate the learning process, orally and in writing.

Developmental Considerations

Keeping in mind that childrens' developmental stages vary, you'll want to adapt the following guidlines to fit the needs of your students.

Children in kindergarten through second grade often have a difficult time maintaining their personal space. Kindergartners, especially, engage in what I call the "Velcro effect"—a mysterious force which sticks them together after you've spent quite a bit of time getting them to sit or stand on their own spots. As you work with them to focus (and as they mature), they are able to maintain their personal space for longer periods of time. Multiple reminders during the movement lessons about maintaining the integrity of their bubbles will help, too.

Young children love the challenge of moving off and then having to find their home base again. They benefit especially from simple, concise, direct commands. Because of their shorter attention spans, you may have to cue each choice when they explore movements, or assign a specific number of times to perform a single action.

Kinders and first and second graders will have difficulty creating their own sequences, but will perform a sequence you have structured. This age group loves creating an "add-on sequence" together as a whole class. In an add-on sequence, students perform a string of contrasting movements from beginning to end each time a movement is added. You usually need to perform the sequence with your students, then you can test their recall by asking them to do the whole sequence without you.

It may take a while for children to become comfortable with finding and investing themselves in their very own movements. At first, some may copy the motion of others. Allow everyone to get comfortable with the work process, then encourage all students to discover their own movements.

In third grade, children are still on the cusp of mastering self-control as movers, yet they are larger and more energetic. They need as much space as possible and plenty of guidelines.

As adolescence approaches and children deal with growth spurts, their awkwardness can look like carelessness. You can help them by reminding them consistently and clearly of spatial awareness parameters. With repetition, fourth, fifth, and sixth graders have no trouble internalizing the abstract concept of personal space. Be sensitive to larger children in the upper grades when giving them space to explore movement. And remember that students can be shy around the opposite gender at this age. Just keep them focused on the movement tasks. Avoid having girls and boys touch, except when it's a part of an engrossing creative problem.

Middle to upper elementary students love increasing physical and sequential challenges. Pile on the tasks in sequences! And remember to encourage clear, expressive movements. Given chunks of time to explore a movement problem, these students can put sequences together either by themselves or in small groups. For example, tell them that they'll have ten minutes to work before demonstrating their sequences. It's a good idea to alert them when they have five, then two minutes left.

Troubleshooting

If students have difficulty paying attention, following directions, or controlling their impulses to interfere with others, give them a warning. Tell them if they cannot improve in those areas, you will ask them to sit down until they are able to rejoin the group. Usually the movement experience proves so enticing, you don't have to follow through on this rule. But sometimes you do.

Dance specialist and educator Susan Cambigue-Tracey invites individuals who cannot participate to become "official observers," and asks them to record the different kinds of movements they observe. She always gives official observers a few minutes to report their observations. Remind observers to describe the kinds of movements, not to comment on how well or poorly various individuals or groups performed. Children who are ill or incapacitated in some way can also be observers and still be involved in the learning process.

Energy. If you have a particularly energetic group, consider progressing into movement experiences incrementally. I start by asking boisterous students to move while seated in their chairs. Then I ask them if they are ready to handle the responsibility of working with more freedom in the space. Usually, students nod their heads eagerly. Then students stand up and work next to their desks. I ask them if they're ready to continue working with a strong focus. Once they concur, I invite them to find a home base, and so on. In this way, they understand that the freedom to move in energetic ways comes with responsibility.

Don't hesitate to stop in the middle of a movement experience if students are not concentrating or are having difficulty controlling their energy. Ask everyone to sit down or lie on the ground and experience passive stillness for one minute. This lowers and refocuses their energy. Then we resume the lesson. Some days you'll find your students are not in the right frame of mind to have a productive and meaningful movement experience. So just stop, move on, then resume working with movement when you sense they can channel their energy effectively.

Unacceptable behavior. Make it absolutely clear from the beginning that intentional shoving or tripping of any kind is unacceptable and will not be tolerated. All students must feel they can move in a safe environment.

Movement Abilities and Limitations

Depending on their age, abilities, disabilities, and backgrounds as movers, students will display a wide range of aptitudes as movers. In movement and dance, we nurture and respect children as expressive beings. We avoid judging or comparing them in terms of physical virtuosity. Except for the profoundly physically disabled, all students can be engaged in movement and dance experiences.

I've helped conduct classes in which children with cerebral palsy were wheeled across a gymnasium floor by classmates while they explored movement ideas with their arms. Hearing-impaired children are astute observers of movement and can understand movement tasks by first observing what their classmates are doing. If they are conversant in American Sign Language, they also have a considerable amount of knowledge to share with classmates as highly expressive communicators. I've worked with learning disabled children whose self-esteem blossomed because they learned how to skip with both sides of their body. Even sight-impaired children, as long as they have defined boundaries and are allowed to explore the area they'll be moving in, can explore movement ideas through verbal prompts.

The key ingredient for progress is *willingness*. Whether they use their hands or whole bodies, students who are willing to explore movement problems and infuse their actions with intention, awareness, knowledge, and feelings, can enhance their physical skills, creativity, and learning. If willing students are having pronounced difficulty with coordination, consult someone who is knowledgeable about anatomy and kinesiology, such as a dancer or physical education teacher, about techniques that can help your students move with more ease and skill.

Students who are willing to infuse their explorations with intention, awareness, knowledge, and feelings, can enhance their physical skills, creativity, and learning.

Injuries or health problems. Sometimes students injure themselves while playing or engaging in sports activities. Any injuries to joints, such as ankles and knees, should be completely healed before students resume movement and dance activities. And if children have internal disorders, such as heart or lung problems, they should get clearance from their physician before they work with full-bodied, energetic movement.

Encouragement. I've found that learners of all ages and abilities are transformed by encouragement. But it must be honest and specific to be effective. Acknowledge shy, inhibited students when they invest themselves fully in a movement problem, overly energetic students who channel their motion more precisely, and your class as a group for improving their ability to move cooperatively with each other.

Problems with Curriculum Content

You'll soon discover that you can easily use movement explorations as assessment tools. Students will show you their oral and reading comprehension as they follow spoken and written commands.

If students seem confused about the curriculum topic you are asking them to investigate through movement, do not hesitate to stop, discuss, and brainstorm any trouble they may be having.

Remember also that movement experiences are supposed to be meaningful and enhancing, not superficial and vague. Just like any other learning experience, movement lessons need to be planned. You'll need to be clear about the lesson's goal and the steps you and your students can take to get there.

Chapter 4

Moving into Understanding

Many years ago, I attended an ecology workshop on an island off the coast of Maine. I learned about geology, different zones of growth, and the dynamic connections between a habitat and its citizens. It was a life-changing experience. I came away with a set of tools that help me understand and appreciate any natural setting I happen to find myself in. This book offers the same kind of tool kit. Learning about dance not only immerses you and your students in a vital discipline, it also equips you to go into any curriculum area and make connections there.

In the creative movement phase, we ask students to explore the elements of dance and exaggerate the size, shape, energy, and timing of their natural movements. Thus, students' movements become more compelling and expressive. It's like learning how to sing instead of speaking in normal conversational tones. Students make more creative choices and connect to curriculum areas in more meaningful ways.

I've divided our work in the creative movement phase into two chapters. In this chapter, you are invited to begin with some basic strategies as you

- lead students in warm-ups that prepare them to move with more variety and skill
- learn more about the elements of dance
- guide fundamental movement explorations and curriculum connections.

In Chapter 5, *Moving into Exploration and Discovery*, you and your students explore the rich connections that are possible between rhythm and design in movement and poetry, geometry, visual arts, and forces in nature.

Working with Sound and Music

Throughout history, music has inspired people to move with focus, grace, power, and imagination. From now on, consider making music and sound sources an integral part of students' learning experiences. At this point, you are not asking students to work directly with music, you are using it to support their efforts.

Wherever possible, I suggest sound sources and music selections as examples. But I urge you to forge your own relationship to music. For assistance, you might consult colleagues who teach music or have a special interest in music.

Be on the lookout for music which has distinctive "moods" but no discernible steady beat or pulse. Much New Age music offers ambient soundscapes—either tranquil or energetic—for students to move in. Consider also using the natural sounds of ocean surf, rainstorms, forests, and whales from environmental recordings. Sound effects recordings have a varied array of mechanical sounds—from clocks ticking, to car motors gunning, to alarms blaring.

Also seek out examples of rhythmic music with a steady beat that you can clap to. Find a variety of pieces with contrasting qualities, such as melodies, speed (tempo), and rhythmic patterns. Expose students to dynamic forms like "world beat"—pop music from Africa, South America, and Asia which fuses non-Western and Western musical forms, as well as traditional American jazz and European classical music.

Building on Prior Knowledge

As educators we know how important it is for students to build on prior knowledge. Before proceeding, be sure your students have experienced the strategies offered in Chapter 3 in which they

- moved in place and through space while aware of personal space
- explored natural movements
- put movement choices into simple sequences.

Getting Smarter about the Body

When students are moving and communicating in out-of-the-ordinary ways with their whole bodies, they'll need to engage in a warm-up. A warm-up prepares the body's muscles and joints to move fully without strain. It's also a way for students to learn about expressive possibilities. They need to get going with large, smooth movements that stretch and bend the body, and then move into isolated movements that make the parts of the body, like the shoulders, arms, torso, and legs, more flexible and articulate.

Moving Safely

To ensure all participants' well-being as movers, you and your students need to know what's right and wrong for the body. What follows are a few pointers that will help everyone move safely.

Protect your lower back. When you lead your students in warm-up movements, lift your abdominal muscles at all times. This will protect your lower back from strain. Take a minute to experience what it feels like to *stand tall*. Imagine you have a string reaching from the middle of your head up toward the ceiling. Lift up the muscles that extend from the top of your legs to your navel. Make the sides of your torso long as well. Remember to keep breathing. You should feel your whole spine get longer. Don't suck in at your navel and tuck your tailbone under you. Instead, let your tailbone *drop down* behind you like it has a heavy rope attached to the end of it. Let your weight drop down through your feet into the ground. Let your shoulders drop as you lift your abdominal muscles and reach out the top of your head. You should feel buoyant and relaxed when you're standing tall.

Respect your body's range of motion. We were constructed to move forward. Our arms and legs and spines have good flexibility in front of us. Hence we have less range of motion to our sides and little to the back of our bodies. While it's useful to maximize the range of movement in those directions, it's important to avoid forcing movements. For instance, never reach your head back and crunch your neck. Forget what some people say about there being no gain without pain. Pain is our body's way of telling us not to do something. Besides encouraging creativity, "finding your own way" to explore a movement problem allows the body to follow its own natural pathways and prevent undue strain.

Environmental safety. The floors of most multi-purpose rooms, gymnasiums, and some classrooms can be extremely hard. If you engage children in vigorous traveling steps such as jumps, make sure they are wearing soft-soled shoes to protect their shins and leg joints—especially their knees. They should bend their knees easily when they come down from jumps—not land stiffly like gymnasts. If you'll be working on a wooden floor you can choose to have children work in bare feet, but never let them move on a slippery tile floor in their socks.

Have all students agree they won't engage in any movement that might hurt themselves or anyone else—like traveling with high energy without watching where they are going, climbing on furniture, and jumping from high places. This should include handstands, back flips, splits, and somersaults.

Point out that these tumbling moves usually take place on thick mats. Challenge students to create movements that no one has ever seen before.

To ensure their comfort while moving, remind children to wear loose, non-restricting clothes on movement and dance days. Remind girls to wear trousers or shorts.

Warm-Ups

There are many ways to warm up our bodies. One way to warm up is to lightly shake parts of our bodies—hands, arms, shoulders, torsos, legs, and feet. Here are two other types of warm-ups in more detail.

Whole body warm-up. Play some peaceful, flute music—like "Haiku" by Deuter, from his *Cicada* recording. Ask students to stretch their whole bodies into the biggest shape they can make. When they've extended their bodies as far as they can, ask them to *contract* ("pull in" for younger children) their bodies into the smallest shape they can make without going off their feet. Have them explore these natural actions several times.

Now you are going to change how they are stretching and contracting their bodies by asking them—at the sound of drum beat—to stretch and contract as *slowly* as they can. Encourage them to find a different way to repeat these actions.

To structure their movements a little, ask them to stretch out in four slow drumbeats and contract in four slow drum beats without stopping. Repeat the stretch-contract cycle four times. Encourage them to find a different way to stretch and contract each time. Tell them they can move their feet and face a different direction on their home bases to discover new ways to stretch and contract.

Now you are going to vary the amount of time in which they move. Ask them to stretch out in two slow drum beats and contract in two drum beats without stopping. Note how this change made the movement speed up and become more energetic. Repeat this three more times.

Ask the whole group if they are ready to meet the challenge of stretching and contracting in only one drum beat. (You should get a lot of excited nods.) Strike the drum once. Students shoot their bodies into a stretched-out shape, then with the next sound cue snap their bodies closed. Repeat several times.

Mirroring body part warm-up. Movement and dance cultivates our ability to move different body parts in isolation. This means a part of the body moves by itself while the rest of the body is still. To experience this, move your shoulders up and down one at a time and make the rest of your body as quiet as possible. You are isolating your shoulders.

Body part warm-ups are designed to warm up and make individual body parts more articulate. One way to focus students, especially younger ones, on isolating different parts of the body is with a strategy called *mirroring*. You may already be familiar with mirroring. It's a simple, yet engrossing activity that encourages students to follow your movements. As the leader, you assume an active role. Your students serve as your mirror, or followers, and spontaneously copy your movements exactly.

Movement and dance cultivates our ability to move different body parts in isolation.

Stand in the front of your classroom and face your students. Have them face you as squarely as possible. Ask them to stand tall on their home bases. To acquaint your students with mirroring, ask them to copy your movements exactly as you bend your arms at the elbow slowly, and lift your lower arms until the palms of your hands face the class. Then, as if standing in a narrow cylinder that permits no forward actions, extend your arms straight up to the ceiling. Make sure your whole class is moving along with you. Lower your arms one at a time. As you lower your right arm, students should be moving their left arms (the proper mirror image) the exact same way, at the the exact same time.

As soon as children understand how this activity works, you can focus on simple up and down actions, or circular motions that loosen up and extend each body part's range of motion. Tip your head gently from side to side, keeping your neck long as you do so. Lift your shoulders up and down several times. Create curves with your arms in front of you, overhead, and to each side.

Once students understand how to isolate their body parts by mirroring your actions, you can step aside and let individual students take over as leader. Or you can ask them to face each other in pairs and alternate roles as leaders and followers. Suggest specific body parts to move—don't forget their elbows, hands, torsos, hips, legs, and feet—and where to move them. Remind children to keep their movements slow and free of strain. They'll soon get the hang of this fun and challenging way to warm-up.

As with so many other movement and dance experiences, mirroring has a host of benefits. It encourages observant leadership by emphasizing the choice of slow and clear movements that classmates can follow easily. While mirroring, students can explore movement problems together, such as how to extend body parts in different directions. Mirroring develops the ability to see and imitate movement. This will come in handy at a later stage when students learn each other's movements, explore the steps of different dance forms, or create dances together.

SHOPTALK

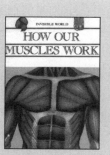

Ávila, Victoria. *How Our Muscles Work.* Illustrated by Antonio Muñoz Tenllado. New York: Chelsea House, 1995.

Walker, Richard. *The Children's Atlas of the Human Body.* Brookfield, Connecticut: The Millbrook Press, 1994.

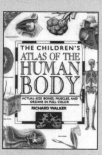

These books are wonderful resources for you and for upper elementary students, too. *How Our Muscles Work* describes in detailed text and illustrations the roles muscles play in basic movements as well as in respiration, circulation, and digestion. *The Children's Atlas of the Human Body* helps you place the muscular and skeletal systems within the context of the whole body. It offers many meaningful connections for kids. Consider having your students study anatomy by investigating the various systems of the body through movement.

The Elements of Dance

Whether students follow your verbal prompts, your movements, or a series of set movements, the warm-up is a short but significant preparation for the heart of the movement and dance experience—learning about the elements of dance.

If you recall, the elements of dance—Space, Energy, and Time—were described earlier as what makes movement more defined and expressive. I pointed out that just as a creative writer draws from a deep pool of words and phrases to express her ideas, so a dance artist needs a varied range of movements from which to choose.

Movement Concepts

Each dance element contains within it movement concepts that make movements specific and distinctive. Read over each concept listed below, as well as the descriptors embedded within each concept. See what comes to mind.

The Elements of Dance

Space	Energy	Time
Size	**Force**	**Speed**
Big	Strong	Slow
Small	Weak	Fast
		Acceleration
Level	**Weight**	Deceleration
High	Heavy	
Medium	Light	**Rhythm**
Low		Natural Time
	Quality	Steady Beat
Shape	Smooth	
Curved	Sharp	
Straight	Swing	
Directions	**Stillness**	
Forward	Active	
Backward	Passive	
Sideways		
Diagonal		
Pathway		
Straight		
Curved		
Circular		
Zig-Zag		
Relationships		
Near		
Apart		

Developing a wide range of movement choices will enable students to make complex curriculum connections and communicate more effectively through movement.

How do your associations compare with the following descriptions?

The element of Space refers to the overall design of movement—both the shapes bodies make, and how the performing space is filled with bodies in motion.

Size describes the range of shapes and movements from small to big. In the whole body warm-up, students extend their bodies into big shapes and make small shapes by contracting all their muscles. Traveling steps come in all sizes.

Students may take very small steps that look like tiny, scurrying runs or they may take very large steps in giant, reaching lunges.

Level describes how high or low movement takes place in relation to the ground. If you recall how students explored their personal space in the last chapter, they reached their arms to the top *(high)* and to the bottom *(low)* of the bubble. In a normal standing position, they are at medium level. Students can execute very high skips across the space, or skips that hover low to the ground.

Shape refers to the designs the body makes in the space. All objects make shapes in the space they are occupying. Shapes are *curved* like an egg, or *straight* like a box, or a combination of both like the letters on this page.

Directions refer to both the directions of the body and the directions in the space. Directions of the body are determined by how you are facing. The front, back, and sides of the body lead us in motion. For example, the *front* of our body propels us *forward* most of the time. Sometimes, if someone steps onto a crowded elevator, we inch *backward* to make room. When we take our seats in a movie theater, we step sideways so we won't trip over anyone's feet.

Directions of the space are determined by which areas of the space we are traveling toward. It doesn't matter which way the body is facing. Students standing on their home bases travel f*orward in the space* by moving toward the "front" of the room (usually where you are standing and giving directions). Whether they skip forward or slide sideways, they are still going *forward in the space*. They travel *backwards in the space* when they return to their home base. If they walk to either side of the room they are moving *sideways in the space*. And when students gesture or travel to the corners of the room they are moving *diagonally in the space*.

Pathway refers to the design of the path made by body parts or the whole body while traveling through space. We usually walk in a *straight* path when traveling down a sidewalk. A child's fingertips trace a *curve* when her arms swing as she skips. Frogs sometimes jump in *zig-zags*. Space shuttles revolve in a circular pathway around the earth.

Relationships describe our proximity to people and things. When children are spread out in a large gymnasium they are moving apart from each other. Students exploring the effects of overpopulation might move *near* each other in a small space. Relationships also encompass all space descriptors like *in front of, behind, to the side of, around, above,* and *below*.

The element of Energy (also known as Force) gives movement varying degrees of expressive intensity by how it is released in motion.

Force describes the amount of energy channeled into our movements. When we chop down a tree, we summon and expend *strong* energy with each stroke of the ax. When we are tired or ill, we lift ourselves out of bed with very *weak* energy.

Weight reflects our relationship to gravity. When we give into gravity, our spines curve, our arms hang, and our steps become plodding. These *heavy* movements can reflect a state of mind like weariness, or help us understand the moves of a massive animal like an elephant. When we resist gravity and move as if we are filled with helium, our movements are *light*. We can express delight through buoyant skips, or understand the weightlessness encountered by travelers in outer space.

Quality refers to the flow of energy in movement. Just as honey drips *smoothly* from a spoon into a teacup, so can we move without any jarring accents. Smooth motion is also known as sustained motion. Invoking the image of slow motion can allow students to understand this movement quality, but it should be noted that *smooth* is not the same as *slow*—that's a concept that belongs in the dance element of **Time**. *Sharp* movement, also known as percussive motion, is the opposite of smooth. Actions are sudden. They are broken into segments that stop and do not flow together. The freeze actions we explored in the previous chapter are sharp movements, as are the alert cocks of a bird's head.

Swing energy is a combination of two kinds of movement related to weight— *collapsed* and *suspended* motion. The pendulum on a grandfather clock, a swing with a child in it, our arms when we walk—all drop down (collapse) then lift up (suspend) when they swing. In dance, swinging motion can be articulated in the arms, legs, upper torso, and whole body.

Stillness refers to the absence of visible motion. *Active stillness* does not move but it's still filled with energy. An egret about to spear a fish is a study in active stillness. Active stillness is the energy we use when engaging in freeze actions. It infuses the sculptures of Rodin and makes the figures come alive. *Passive stillness* refers to the absence of motion and animating energy. Letting all the energy drain out of the body while either sitting or lying down produces a very relaxed sensation. If you recall, I recommended using passive stillness with your students to help them relax and refocus their energy.

The element of Time refers to how fast or slow movement is, and how it unfolds rhythmically.

Speed is like *tempo* in music and refers to the rate at which movements occur. Gazelles run very *fast*, while a turtle's locomotion on land is very *slow*. Cars driving onto a freeway *accelerate* to catch up with the flow of traffic, then *decelerate* to exit the off-ramp safely.

In dance, students make inventive choices on the spot as they explore specific movement problems.

Rhythm refers to the dynamic patterns with which movement unfolds. *Natural time* characterizes movements that happen in their own natural flow. A bubbling brook travels down a hillside in natural time. A bird will swoop from branch to branch in natural time. While investigating natural movement, students were cued to work with movements of various lengths at their own speed.

There are two ways to work with a *steady beat*. In the looser version, students move in their own way within a certain number of drumbeats. Remember how students traveled off then returned to their home bases in sixteen drums beats? When working with a steady beat as it relates to music, movements fall with the framework of a pulse, and take place within a set number of beats.

Movement Exploration

Remember how your students chose their own movements to establish their personal space? how they put action words into motion, and explored the versatility of body parts while warming up? Creative problem solving is the key that unlocked the door to their sense of discovery as learners and creators.

Students learn about the elements of dance the same way. They explore and solve problems using movements based on concepts drawn from the elements of Space, Energy, and Time. They engage in a focused yet open-ended process called movement exploration, also known as *improvisation*. When students improvise in drama, they use their imaginations to make choices on the spot within a given situation. In dance, students make inventive choices on the spot as they explore specific movement problems. In both instances, students are given the opportunity to explore a range of possibilities.

Experiencing a Movement Concept

The best way to understand a movement exploration is to experience one. The following movement concept—*weight*—is drawn from the dance element of Energy. You are invited to explore it using your arms. Even if you decide not to try it, be sure to read through this section to get acquainted with the exploration process.

Here we go. Wherever you are sitting, right now, lift your arm up easily, then lower it down easily. Good. Try the same natural movement with your other arm.

Lift both your arms up, then, like a boat filling slowly with water, let them sink back down to your lap. What made your arms sink? Yes, it's gravity, the force that keeps our feet on the ground by exerting a constant pull on us. Find different ways to lift and lower your arms exaggerating how heavy your arms feel coming down.

What's the opposite of heavy? Solve another movement problem to find out. Discover motion that defies gravity—as if you are a balloon filling up with helium. Do your movements feel weightless? light? As you find different ways to lift your arm up with light, buoyant energy, can your arm make a pathway made out of curved lines? What about speed? Can your arms fill up with light energy quickly?

Put the two kinds of energy together into a short sequence. Using one or both arms, lift up with light energy and sink down with heavy energy three times. As you experience heavy and light energy, explore different pathways for your arms, and experiment with different speeds.

You have just experienced the essence of a movement exploration in movement and dance. Here's a recap of all that took place.

- You responded to my commands and found your own ways to put them into action.
- You started with natural movement—lifting and lowering your arms—then were asked to change *how* you lifted and lowered your arms by becoming conscious of your relationship to gravity.
- You were encouraged to find different ways to lift and lower your arms with light and heavy energy. Doing this enabled you to learn about heavy and light motion through a process of discovery.
- While you focused on the dance element of Energy, you also used concepts from the other elements to change or vary how you explored heavy and light energy. Integrating your heavy and light movements with awareness of speed and pathway made the motion more defined and distinctive.

Students can follow a similar process to learn about any of the movement concepts embedded in the elements of dance. Whatever the movement concept, each exploration follows the same basic progression. Students

- warm-up
- explore a movement concept in place and/or through space
- create a culminating sequence.

Learning about Size

Asking students to explore the extremes of big and little shapes and movements is a simple but effective way to help them step outside the range of natural movement.

Suggested music. Selections from Gabrielle Roth's "Body Jazz" section on her *Initiation* recording.

Warm-up. Once students have established their personal space, engage them in the shaking body part warm-up. Ask them to make their shakes very small to begin with, then gradually increase the size. Then engage students in a whole body warm-up. Growing from very small to very big, and back again to very small, reinforces their understanding of size.

Movement exploration—in place. Ask students to find three big shapes they can move into and freeze in. Give older students a few minutes to explore various big shapes, then ask them to choose three. Children may go on the floor to find big shapes. This works well with a clean, safe floor.

Ask them to move into each *big* shape at the sound of a sharp drum beat. Play three sharp drum beats to cue their moves into three large shapes. Next, have students investigate different small shapes. Then have students move into the three big shapes and three *small* shapes without stopping. Repeat this sequence. For extra challenge and contrast, ask them to alternate between a big shape and a small shape every time they hear the beat of a drum. Remind them to find a different shape each time.

Through space. Ask students to count off into 1s and 2s. 1s take sixteen *tiny* walks as they move off of and return to their home base. 2s freeze on their home bases in large shapes while 1s travel. Then reverse roles. Next, ask 1s to take four *large* walks off and four *large* walks back to their home base while 2s freeze in small shapes. Reverse roles.

Culminating sequence. Students coalesce what they've learned and are given the opportunity to experience a series of varied movements without stopping the flow of motion.

Primary grade sequence:

> Grow into a big shape on home base in four slow beats.
>
> Take eight tiny walks off home base.
>
> Take four large walks back to home base.
>
> Pull into a tiny shape on home base in four slow beats.

Upper grade sequence:

> Grow from a small to a large shape in four slow beats.
>
> Travel with eight tiny walks off home base.
>
> Travel with four large walks back to home base.
>
> Make one small shape/one large shape/one small shape at the sound of single, sharp drum beats.

Ask a small group of students to volunteer and model the sequence while everyone else watches carefully. To make it easier for the group that is demonstrating the sequence, give them one set of directions at a time. Making corrections or adjustments with this group will help the whole class.

As the 1s and 2s go the first time, you'll probably have to call out the directions or count out each part of the four-part sequence. Then challenge the students to show you the sequence cued only by drum beats. Allow each group to repeat the sequence several times without stopping so they can invest themselves in the overall flow of the sequence.

Variation. Ask students to explore other traveling steps—jumps, hops, skips—of different sizes as they travel off then back to their home bases.

Learning Level, Speed, Force, and Weight

In a moment, we'll examine how to connect movement concepts to learning across the curriculum. Right now it's important to continue building your students' knowledge of dance by immersing them in the movement concepts of level, speed, force, and weight.

Not only are these fundamental movement concepts easily understood, but we can use size, level, and speed to enrich the exploration of other movement concepts. Developing this wide range of movement choices will enable students to make complex curriculum connections and communicate more effectively through movement.

Repetition

After students get comfortable with a movement task, repetition becomes anessential ingredient of all successful movement explorations. Repetition

deepens the learning experience and

- enables students to experiment with different movement choices
- promotes students' "muscle memory" of the concepts being explored
- enables you to coach students to make their movements more specific and become skilled as movers.

How much repetition is enough? Your own students will tell you what they need depending on their age and experience. In general, they'll need to experience movements and movement sequences at least two to three times. To focus your K-2 students, you'll want to cue them for every movement choice they make. Give your older children a few minutes to find different ways of exploring a specific problem. You'll see students find movements in their own way and at their own rate.

Aesthetic awareness. In the following learning events, be sure students experience the extremes of each movement concept they explore. Ask them to make their movements as low or high, small or large, slow or quick, strong or weak, heavy or light as possible.

Learning about level
Students follow a progression similar to that used in the exploration of size to learn about different levels in space.

Movement exploration in place. Have students explore shapes at ground level (low), standing level (medium), and with their bodies as far away from the ground as they can, while remaining on their feet (high). Here's a helpful image: ask them to sit or crouch at a low level and imagine the ceiling has been lowered to just a few inches above their heads. Encourage them to discover all the shapes they can make at this level. Then raise the ceiling so they can stand at medium level to find shapes. Then put the ceiling back to where it was so they can find shapes that reach high into the space. Direct students to choose one shape at each level that they can move into quickly. Have them move into each shape in two slow beats. For contrast, cue each shape with a sharp drum beat.

Through space. Ask students to travel away from, then back to their home bases with low traveling steps (which can include movements such as crawls if the floor surface is safe). Have them explore high traveling steps by reaching their upper bodies towards the ceiling and walking on their tiptoes.

Culminating sequence. With your help, students can create a culminating sequence which includes low, medium, and high shapes in place, together with low and high steps through space.

Time/Speed

Movement which is very slow or quick feels and looks very different from movement that flows at normal speeds. It also requires physical control. Students find it challenging to exaggerate quickness or slowness in movement.

See what happens if you ask students to get up from their seats, then slide their chairs under their tables or desks in *slow* motion. They become aware of certain details in movement that we all take for granted, like how it feels to shift our weight from being seated to standing on two legs.

To explore the extremes of *quick* motion, ask students to walk away from, then back to their home bases as quickly as they can. Challenge them to maintain the clarity and size of their movements while they are moving quickly. Tell them to pay particular attention to focusing on where they are moving so they avoid bumping into anyone or anything.

Energy/Force and Weight

Everything that moves in the universe is animated by energy, yet everything does not move in the same way. Rocket ships, smoke, and panthers make their way through space with different degrees of strength. Human beings, submarines, and birds have different relationships with gravity which keeps them tethered to the earth. The movement concepts of *force* and *weight* from the dance element of Energy offer students rich areas of discovery as movers, learners, and creators.

Imagery. One of the most vital ways to help students understand different kinds of movement is to use imagery. While exploring light movement in your arms, you were asked to raise your arms "as if you are a balloon filling up with helium." That image helped support your understanding of the concept. In movement and dance, great care is given to how we work with imagery. If we emphasize *being* the imagery, children may get tangled up in its content, and miss the embedded movement ideas. For instance, if you started a movement exploration of heavy motion with your class by saying, "Imagine you are a drop of water sliding down the side of a glass," your students might start thinking about the shape and motion of this droplet and fail to consider how this image could inspire them to move with a sense of heaviness.

By simply inserting the words *move as if* or *move like* when you use imagery, you help students focus on themselves as movers who are using imagery to explore different kinds of motion. Since they are not tied to a specific image, they can use their movement knowledge to make connections across the curriculum.

Strong and Weak Energy

Strong and weak energy are the results of how much *force* we use in movements. An enjoyable and challenging way for students to understand strong and weak energy is to connect to the dynamics of music.

Select any piece of music. You can turn the volume up and down to guide your students' movements. Or, to make a more explicit connection to dynamics in music, choose a piece of music which demonstrates forceful and soft dynamics like the Adagio-allegro molto section of Dvořák's Symphony no. 9 ("New World").

Ask students to stand on their home bases. When they hear forceful music, invite them to move any way they want inside their bubble or spaceship with loud movement—energetic motion that announces itself strongly. Insist that no one make a sound with their voices or feet. Encourage them to explore movements of different sizes, levels, speeds, and to turn around inside their personal space. Label this movement "strong."

When they hear softer music, ask them to explore the opposite energy by moving in their bubble or spaceship with quiet or weak movements. Students should be moving with less intensity. Encourage them to explore movements of different sizes, levels, and speeds.

Visual resources. As you will see in the following lesson on heavy and light energy, visual resources like objects, videos, photographs, graphics, charts, books, and student artwork can support your students' movement explorations. Visual resources that demonstrate motion are the most powerful. Remember, you are supporting students' understanding of the kind of motion being demonstrated and sparking their imaginations, you are not inviting them to impersonate the object or forces they are investigating.

Learning Event

Heavy and Light Energy

Introduction. Focus students on what they will be learning. To understand the movement concept of weight, students will explore the impact of gravity on their body weight. Giving in to gravity will make their movements heavy. Defying this force will infuse their movements with light energy.

Suggested music. The title cut from Steve Roach's *Structures from Silence*.

Warm-up. Have students do a whole body warm-up emphasizing lightness when they stretch and heaviness when they contract their bodies.

Movement exploration—in place. Have students crouch in a low shape. Blow up a balloon. Ask them to follow the motion of the balloon as you do so. Students expand into a *large, light shape*. Tie the balloon so air cannot escape. Tap the balloon gently into the air and ask students to put the movements of the balloon into their bodies while still remaining on their home bases. Ask them how they would describe this movement. Try to establish the word "light" or any other synonyms.

Explain that you are going to ask them to explore the *opposite* of light energy. (Ask older students to show you what the opposite of light energy would look like.) Students should stand with their fingertips extended to the ceiling. Ask them to sink *slowly* all the way down to the ground. They should use their hands to help ease themselves into a sitting position, or if the floor is safe and clean, a lying position on the floor.

Ask them what this kind of movement felt and looked like and label this movement "heavy."

Through space. Divide students up into 1s and 2s. While 1s sit in heavy, low shapes, ask 2s to take four large, heavy steps off home base and freeze. Ask them to fill up with light energy and float back to home base in four slow drum beats. When they return to home base, direct them to make a large, light turn in place then drop and freeze into a heavy shape.

Ask 1s to do the same. Then ask 1s and 2s to each repeat the sequence without freezing.

Variation. Have each group repeat the sequence changing the *speeds* of their movements. For example, have them experiment with taking quick, heavy steps off home base, then slow floating steps back, ending with a quick light turn. Have both groups repeat the whole sequence several times.

Challenge. In movement explorations, use your well-developed kidwatching awareness to gauge when your students are losing focus. Sometimes all they need is a greater challenge—one that can meet and channel their high level of energy.

- Ask students to involve the whole body in movement choices, and to make their movements more defined and unlike anyone else's.
- As they explore, alternate back and forth between opposites so students are challenged by contrasts.
- When students layer several variations all at once (large, light, fast walks), ask them to clearly show each movement concept they include.

Cool Down

After a vigorous movement experience, students need to shift into energy that is appropriate for other activities. As I mentioned in the description of passive stillness earlier, in a cool down students close their eyes and drain the tension out of all their muscles while sitting or lying down. Challenge them to be absolutely still for one minute. Look at your watch or the wall clock to conduct this experiment in real time.

After a vigorous movement experience, students need to shift into energy that is appropriate for other activities.

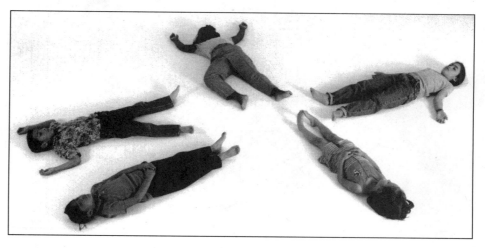

You may need to direct individual students to close their eyes or stop fidgeting. Do this quietly and gently. Remember they are rarely asked to be still this way. Experiencing stillness for one minute can help children achieve a peaceful state that is both refreshing and relaxing.

Observation and Reflection

As you discovered while working with natural movement, students can deepen their learning by observing each other's efforts. Then you can ask students to label the kinds of movements they saw, describe what the sequences made them think of, and point out any especially compelling moments. (See page 49 in Chapter 3 for Viewing Guidelines.)

Journals. Give students an opportunity to write in their dance journals. The act of capturing what they did and saw as movers and creators in words will not only strengthen their learning, it will sharpen their articulation skills as well. Have them also reflect on their progress by answering questions such as:

- What movements did I like doing best?
- What was difficult for me?
- What do I need to work on to grow as a mover?
- What would I change about today's experience?
- What would I like to learn about next?

Your own reflection. Be sure to ask yourself reflection questions such as:

- What have I learned about teaching movement and dance?
- How can I apply what I have learned to the next lesson?
- When were my students most involved? Why?
- What parts were most difficult? Why?
- What do students need to learn next?

The more consistently your students move, the more movement and dance knowledge they can retain and apply.

Timeline

The learning events which focus on a movement concept are designed to take place in approximately thirty minutes. Some of the upcoming learning events which include a curricular connection need at least forty-five minutes. The first few times out, I recommend you choose to concentrate on a movement lesson *without* a curriculum connection so that you and your students can focus fully on the movement concept being explored. You can then engage children in a follow-up lesson that reviews the movement material from the preceding lesson and emphasizes the curriculum connection. Remember, the more consistently your students move, the more movement and dance knowledge they can retain and apply.

Connections across the Curriculum

Great ideas originate in the muscles.

Thomas Edison

Dance as a Way of Knowing offers several approaches to integrating dance concepts with other areas of learning. Students can

- use their dance knowledge to deepen their understanding of single topics, concepts, and processes in other disciplines
- integrate dance with other curricular areas and communicate what they've learned through movement.

Whatever the curriculum focus, students can investigate topics or ideas through their kinesthetic intelligence. Only now, their knowledge of different dance concepts will allow them to make more specific, in-depth connections. For instance, students can use their knowledge of heavy and light movement to explore the impact of gravity in different environments.

Learning about Gravity

Have students create a sequence of natural movements which involves labor—unloading the back of a truck, for example, or building a shelter. Ask them to enact the sequence with particular sensitivity to weight. This means they experience and show the relative weights of objects and actions they are working with.

Once students have created the sequence of movement and can perform it without stopping, ask them to exaggerate the size of their movements. Remember, even though the main focus is on heavy and light energy, they can use other movement concepts to vary and enhance their movement choices.

Then ask them to imagine they are in a weightless environment. A good visual resource is video footage of astronauts on the moon. Ask them to explore what happens to their actions when the pull of gravity is much weaker.

For contrast, ask them to explore what would happen to their actions if they were in an environment with double the pull of earth's gravity. Challenge them to make their movements strong as well as heavy as they push against the force of gravity.

Ask students what they learned about the force of gravity through watching each other's sequences. What kinds of movements communicated the relative presence or absence of gravitational forces?

Language arts. Students can create "movement phrases" based on action words, as well as time and energy descriptors. For example, they can

- skip quickly with light energy
- saunter slowly with heavy energy.

Have students explore their own movement phrases while traveling off then back to home base. Have them write down their phrase, exchange with a classmate, then translate each other's movement phrases in their own imaginative way. Be sure to have students watch each other's movement choices so they can observe the distinctions in movement and meaning.

Social studies and science. Students can discover how animals move. Very often students have a general idea of how animals move, but their understanding is limited because they are not conscious of an animal's size, the size of its movements, its relationship to the ground, or its speed, power, or weight, except through words they may have heard or read, or static images they may have seen. Grasping the spatial and energetic dimensions of animal movement kinesthetically offers students another way of knowing these creatures.

Grasping the spatial and energetic dimensions of animal movement kinesthetically offers students another way of knowing these creatures.

Establish the animal's habitat and its impact on the animals' movement. Determine the type of traveling step (crawl, spring, soar, prowl) the animal uses. With smaller, legless creatures like snakes and fish, students can travel on their feet to explore the actions of their animal with their torsos, arms, and hands. Ask students to identify, in place, the basic size, level, and speed with which their animal moves. Then ask them to determine the relative strength and weight of the animal's movements.

Challenge students to discover and select the movements which best capture the essence of each animal. This will help students identify the animal's unique characteristics. For instance, to communicate the essence of a penguin a student might choose quick waddling walks punctuated by pokes of the head. The trajectory of a butterfly might include light flutters of the hands in graceful arcs. Students can demonstrate the movements they've chosen by traveling off then back to their home bases in sixteen drum beats.

Did students learn anything surprising or new about animals by watching each other's movements? Ask them to write about why they chose certain movements to communicate the essence of their animal.

SHOPTALK

Joyce, Mary. *First Steps in Teaching Creative Dance to Children.* 2d ed. Mountain View, California: Mayfield Publishing, 1980.

——. *Dance Technique for Children.* Mountain View, California: Mayfield Publishing, 1984.

Mary Joyce is a highly-regarded children's dance educator. *First Steps in Teaching Creative Dance to Children* features lessons based on the elements of dance and is a helpful introduction to working with movement. The lessons are presented in the first person as if she is speaking with students, yet the progressions are clear. Use this book to guide your students in deeper explorations of the elements of dance. It offers concrete strategies she calls "helpers," as well as photographs of children solving movement problems.

If you want to help your students develop their physical skills, consult *Dance Technique for Children.* Engaging lessons help children develop their awareness of how to move the whole body and body parts in healthy, refined, and articulate ways. It includes a wonderful section on traveling steps (locomotor forms).

Integrating More Than One Discipline

Besides deepening their knowledge of specific curricular areas, students can synthesize knowledge from several curricular areas and communicate what they know through creative movements.

The Legend of the Medicine Wheel

To demonstrate, I offer a sequence of strategies I used with a third-grade class, in collaboration with their teacher, Pam Strain, at Emma W. Shuey Elementary School in Rosemead, California. The students combined their knowledge of social studies, dance, science, and language arts to make a group movement study which expressed what they knew and felt about animals from a Native American legend called *The Legend of the Medicine Wheel,* a tale from the Plains Indians that explains their all-encompassing philosophy.

After you grasp the following progression, select your own rich literature resources which focus on animals to use with your students.

Timeline. Four movement sessions.

Suggested music. Selections from *Emergence; Songs of the Rainbow World* by R. Carlos Nakai.

The workspace. These strategies work best in an open space like a multi-purpose room, but students can work in a cleared classroom for the first two sessions. In a best-case scenario, try to schedule time in a multi-purpose room for all four sessions.

The text.

> The wheel is a circle that contains all things: you, me, the animals, the earth. It is divided into four basic directions: North, South, East, and West with Mother Earth and Father Sky. Each direction is linked to a specific animal, color, and attribute. Native People believed that we come into this world at a certain point on the circle, and that in order to become "whole," we must travel full circle and experience the other directions.
>
> *South*: The mouse is a small animal that comes from the south. He lives close to the earth and reflects a feeling of innocence. His color is that of the grass—green, new, alive with growth. He scurries about and does not see much beyond his own home. He has small eyes but a big heart.
>
> *East*: The eagle soars from the east and lives high in the sky near the sun. Because he flies far from the ground his eyes are strong. He sees far and wide. His color is the color of illumination—like the rays of the rising, sparkling, vibrant sun.
>
> *North*: In the north lives the buffalo, a wise creature. The people understood his wisdom for he sacrificed his hide for their houses and clothing, his meat for their hunger, and his bones for their utensils. And the people never wasted any part of this animal, for they knew how precious a gift it was. They showed their thanks by never taking more than they needed. The buffalo is white—a white that contains all the colors of the rainbow—for his wisdom embraces all.
>
> *West*: In the west is found the bear, hibernating in the quiet darkness of his cave. Like his cave, his color is black. He sits quietly gathering his strength through deep introspective thought.
>
> Excerpt from *Exploring Curriculum Ideas through Dance*, produced by Susan Cambigue-Tracey for Performing Tree, 1985. Native American Artist—Kai Ganado. Printed by permission of Susan Cambigue-Tracey.

Connecting to the text. During each session, a group of students can read the text aloud so that everyone can focus on what the words describe and mean to them. As you can see, the legend is loaded with rich action words and phrases like *scurries, alive with growth,* and *soars.* Other phrases such as *sits quietly gathering his strength* and *the rays of the rising, sparkling, vibrant sun* help us see the unique energy radiating from each animal.

First session. Have the whole class sit in a large circle. Ask small groups of five to six students to assemble one group at a time, in the center of the circle. Guide them to explore big and small shapes and movements as they travel in and around each other for eight drums beats. Then guide students to explore the specific actions of the mouse, eagle, buffalo, and bear.

A general reminder: even though students are being asked to move simultaneously in small groups, they should be guided to find their own way to express their understanding of how each animal moves.

Between sessions have students research the animals through texts, photographs, and, if possible, videotapes. Also have students investigate the role of each animal in the lives of the Plains Indians. How were they dependent on each animal? What did each animal symbolize?

Second session. Acquaint your students with movements that reach high and low, both in place (eight drum beats) and while traveling through the space (sixteen drum beats). Ask them to connect their knowledge of moving low and high to the actions of the mouse, eagle, buffalo and bear, while moving in place and through space.

Between sessions investigate the directions of the globe—South, East, North, West—as they relate to your classroom. Divide your class into the four animal groups.

Third session. Establish the global directions as they relate to the multi-purpose room. Each animal group should assemble according to the direction their animal comes from: South (mouse); East (eagle); North (buffalo); West (bear). Ask each animal group to review the size and level of their animal's movements as they travel in and around each other for sixteen drum beats. Then have them investigate the relative weight and power of their animal. Encourage them also to infuse their movements with responses to the attributes of these animals described in the text. Ask each group to "sketch" movements which capture the essence of their animal within sixteen drum beats.

Fourth session. Guide students into the following culminating sequence:

- The whole class stands in a large circle with one student reading the introductory passage of the legend.
- Another student reads the passage that pertains to the mouse; the group communicating the attributes of the mouse walks to the center

of the circle in eight drum beats; they present movements they discovered together in sixteen drum beats and freeze in their last shape; they resume their places in the circle in eight drum beats.

- Each of the remaining groups follows this sequence.

Unique expression. Notice how deeply responsive each child is to the essence of the animal. One child may infuse the movements of the eagle with her own vibrancy as she glides with light, graceful steps and a strong focus. Another child may connect to the wisdom of the buffalo through the proud bearing of his shoulders, the strength of his gallops, and the calm, serious expression on his face. This is the magical, mysterious heart of self-expression which makes each child's movements unique.

Reflection. Ask students to write in their dance journals and describe what they experienced and observed as they created and presented their group project. Ask them what they learned about the Plains Indians by engaging in this movement project.

 Portrait of a Creative Mover at the Basic Level
Let's examine another portrait of a mid-level elementary student— a creative mover who understands basic concepts in dance.

Participation. The student is able to move in place and through space while remaining sensitive to his or her personal space and the space and efforts of others. The student knows how to work effectively by him or herself, with a partner, and with a group; is able to reflect on his or her experience and progress.

Movement. The student articulates different body parts as well as the whole body; solves a movement problem while exploring movement in place (axial) and movement through space (locomotor); selects, then sequences movements; integrates various movement concepts simultaneously.

Aesthetic awareness. *As a mover:* the student demonstrates movements of various sizes, levels, speeds, force and weight; generates original movements while exploring different movement concepts; invests movements with imaginative, authentic responses; and performs sequences with a sustained sense of flow. *As an observer:* the student is able to identify and label different movement concepts and to articulate his or her understanding of the creative movements of others.

Curriculum content. The student demonstrates knowledge of single topics, such as how gravity affects body weight in different environments, as well as action words and descriptors. The student is able to synthesize learning from several disciplines—social studies, science, language arts, and dance— and communicate knowledge through expressive sequences of movement.

While the same developmental considerations mentioned in Chapter 3 apply, if you've worked consistently with movement, your students—whatever their age—are more experienced in the movement exploration process as well as the process of discovering curriculum connections.

You are becoming a seasoned facilitator of movement and dance experiences. Now you're ready to transfer this knowledge to more richly faceted learning experiences.

DIALOGUE

Design a movement experience in which students explore and show what they know about the concept of "opposites."

Where will my students move? Will they move on their own spots in available classroom space? in a cleared classroom? in a multi-purpose room?

_____

_____

How will they connect to the concept of opposites? Will they explore the movement concepts themselves? How can they synthesize their knowledge from different disciplines?

_____

_____

How will students consolidate their learning and show what they know about opposites?

_____

_____

What questions will guide students's observation of each other's work and reflection?

_____

_____

Chapter 5

Moving into Exploration and Discovery

Discovery consists of looking at the same thing as everyone else and thinking something different.

Albert Szent-Gyorgyi

In this chapter, you and your students are invited to explore movement concepts and creative strategies which lie at the heart of dance. As you move to a steady beat and work with the design concepts of shape and pathway, you'll discover connections to diverse curriculum areas such as metered poetry, geometry, forces in nature, and mapping journeys.

I invite you to focus on guiding these rich content connections. As you implement them, be sure to include a warm-up, time for exploration and observation, a cool-down, and questions for reflection.

Moving to a Steady Beat

Thus far, your students have moved either in their own natural time or within the loose confines of a certain number of drum beats. Moving to a steady beat lays the foundation for understanding the unique partnership that exists between music and dance in all cultures. It also gives students the tools they need to make vital connections to language arts.

Feeling a Steady Beat

Take your pulse. After you locate your pulse on the inside of your wrist, feel how it beats at regular intervals for a moment or two. Tap your foot or nod your head to reinforce your awareness of the pulse's steadiness. Now let go of your pulse and see if you can tap your foot or nod your head with the same steadiness without changing the speed. The next time you hear a lively piece of music, tap your foot or put a gentle bounce in your knees. Better yet, put the steady beat into different parts of the body with small movements. Bear in mind that just as our hearts beat at different rates, so does music have steady beats of different speeds. A lively polka is faster than a fox-trot. Whatever the speed, or *tempo* of the regular beat, practice counting or tapping it out for at least a minute or two.

The dashes below represent a steady beat, like your heart beat or the pulsing beat you'd find in a piece of music. Why not play music that has a strong steady beat? "Ja Funmi" from Nigerian Juju artist King Sunny Ade's *Juju Music* recording would work well while you read through this section.

Moving to a steady beat lays the foundation for understanding the unique partnership that exists between music and dance in all cultures.

— — — — — — — — — — — — —

Put on this recording, or another example of music with a lively rhythm, and let yourself move to the steady beat. For now, move on every beat. Clap your hands.

Keep moving and playing with the beat. Put it somewhere else besides your hands and feet.

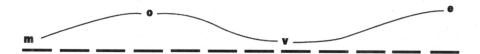

Keep going. Feel the steadiness and the buoyancy. Now change *how* you are moving. Do something different with the beat. Try one long *smooth* move. This is called *moving through* the beat.

Then go back to moving on every beat. Never stop feeling the steady beat.

move	move	move	move	move	move	move	move	move	move	move	move

Try a few sharp moves on different beats. Chapter 4 describes sharp energy, if you need a reminder. Then try moving with sharp energy (punch the air) on one beat and freezing for several beats after. This is called *holding through the beat.*

sharp move	hold	hold	hold	hold	sharp move	hold	hold	sharp move	hold	hold	hold

Now take a few minutes to play with these different ways of moving to a steady beat.

- *move on* each beat
- *move through* the beat with smooth energy
- *move sharply* on one beat then *hold through*

Put them together to make a long, varied rhythmic pattern.

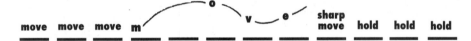

Steady Beat/Rhythmic Pattern

Gather students in a circle in a cleared space. Play some lively music that has a moderate tempo, such as "Montaña" from *The Best of the Gipsy Kings* recording. Then ask students to move on every beat by clapping.

Students can put this beat in different parts of their bodies as a little warm-up. Go from the head right down to the feet. Encourage them to bounce in their knees gently as they put the beat in different body parts.

Explain to students that they're going to play a follow-the-leader game to help them understand rhythmic patterns. You are going to move and you'd like them to echo your movements.

Clap four times.

Take four marching steps.

march   march   march   march
___ ___ ___ ___

Lift and lower your shoulders for four beats.

lift   lower   lift   lower
___ ___ ___ ___

Move to a steady beat, in different ways, to create rhythmic patterns for your students to echo back.

Lift your arms with smooth energy for four beats.

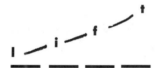

Punch the air in front of you with your elbow and hold for three beats.

punch   hold   hold   hold
___ ___ ___ ___

Students should echo your movements as well as your rhythmic patterns as accurately as possible. Repeat these kinds of rhythmic patterns until everyone is comfortable with them. (Return to moving on each beat when everyone needs to reconnect to its steadiness.) Once students have experienced echoing back the short patterns you have made up, go around the circle so that each child can have a turn creating a rhythmic pattern for four beats that everyone echoes back.

Rhythmic Patterns for Upper Grades

Once you see that students can relate their movements to a steady beat and can come up with simple patterns, challenge them to create more complex, dynamic rhythmic patterns. Then they can divide up into groups, teach each other their movement patterns, and create one long group pattern.

Play any kind of pulsing, rhythmical music such as Nigerian drummer Babatunde Olatunji's "Gin-Go-Lo-Ba," from his *Olatunji! Drums of Passion* recording. First, ask students to work by themselves to create an eight-beat movement pattern that draws upon their response to the music. Encourage them to use their knowledge of size, level, force, weight, and quality to make dynamic movement choices.

Have students divide into groups of four and teach each other their movement patterns. Then ask students to arrange their patterns into a thirty-two beat movement sequence that each group will perform in unison.

Guidelines for Collaboration

Since this is the first time students are being asked to collaborate, not just move together, have them articulate some agreements about how to work together. General ground rules might include

- everyone understands the task
- all contributions are treated with respect
- everyone decides what's most effective for the group project.

Consider also whether individuals should have designated roles like that of leader and timekeeper.

Students are being asked to collaborate, not just move together, so have them articulate some agreements about how to work together.

You and your students can develop more specific guidelines for each movement assignment. For instance, students will have to choose the order of their rhythmic patterns. This can be done by chance—students draw numbers 1-2-3-4 and arrange their patterns accordingly—or through some other arbitrary ordering device like the alphabetical order of their last names. If students are experienced movers and observers, they can watch each other's patterns, then exercise their critical thinking skills to select an order which would create the most compelling group pattern.

Practice and presentation. Give students time to learn and practice performing their rhythmic patterns. Then have each group present their work. Ask observers to point out the ways the movement patterns offer variety and interest.

Connecting to other subjects. Students can explore connections between their movement patterns, and patterns in math and visual arts by drawing visual representations of their movement patterns. Creating dynamic rhythmic patterns also lays the groundwork for learning about dance forms like those from African, Caribbean, and Latin American cultures, in which music and dance are inseparable and rhythmically complex.

Rhythm in Language

Students can connect to rhythm in language by exploring metered poetry through movement.

Primary grades can work with nursery rhymes. Ask your class to read or recite "Peas, Porridge, Hot" with you.

> Peas, porridge, hot
> Peas, porridge, cold
> Peas, porridge, in the pot
> Nine days old.

Have everyone establish a moderate underlying beat by clapping with you. Then have everyone recite or read the poem while still clapping. Increase the challenge by speaking and clapping the rhythm of the first line at the same time. Have students echo back the words and claps. Repeat this several times. Work with the next three lines the same way. Then ask the students to recite and clap the patterns of the lines of the poem without stopping. Are they ready to step the rhythm out with their feet?

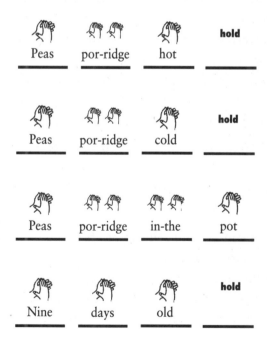

Students can show you the rhythm with other body movements as well. As a final challenge, ask them to "swallow the words" of the poem and show you the poem either with steps or body parts, without reciting the words out loud.

Field Notes: Teacher-To-Teacher

I use nursery rhymes like "Peas, Porridge, Hot" to help my students understand the rhythm of language. First I read the nursery rhyme to my first graders so they're familiar with it. Then students extend it into movement by feeling the beat and the rhythm of the words in their bodies. We move using different body parts in place and across the floor several different ways, until I see they understand the rhythm of the nursery rhyme. I can see that when children understand the rhythm of language it helps them read—movement brings us one step closer.

Ron Aschieris
Savannah Elementary School
Rosemead, California

Upper grades can put a poem like "Spaghetti" by Shel Silverstein, from *Where the Sidewalk Ends,* into motion.

> *Spaghetti, spaghetti all over the place,*
> *Up to my elbows—up to my face,*
> *Over the carpet and under the chairs,*
> *Into the hammock and wound round the stairs,*
> *Filling the bathtub and covering the desk,*
> *Making the sofa a mad mushy mess.*
> *The party is ruined, I'm terribly worried,*
> *The guests have all left (unless they're all buried).*
> *I told them, "Bring presents." I said, "Throw confetti."*
> *I guess they heard wrong*
> *'Cause they all threw spaghetti!*

Before you work with your students, read over the poem to yourself several times. You may notice it has a swinging feeling. Start swaying easily and swing your arms from side to side as you speak the poem out loud. Then clap out the rhythm of each line as you speak it.

Write the poem on the chalkboard so everyone can read it. Then ask students to stand on their home bases and sway gently. Have students read the poem with you as they sway to the underlying beat. Repeat this until the group is speaking fairly clearly in unison.

Use the follow-the-leader format to challenge them to speak and clap the rhythm of each line at the same time. You clap and say one line. They echo back, clapping and speaking the line. Then ask them to articulate the rhythm with movement other than clapping, one line at a time. Students can step out the rhythm or move body parts. (They'll stop swaying.)

As a final challenge, ask them to "swallow the words" and articulate the rhythm of the poem through movement, as a whole group, without reciting it out loud. Allow them to read the poem off the chalkboard since they will not have had time to memorize it. Ask them to identify the action words and space descriptors. Encourage them to find movements that reflect the meaning of the poem, but are still rhythmically accurate.

The design concept of shape makes dance movement defined and distinctive.

Observation. Divide the group in half. Have one group move while the other group watches and recites the poem silently to themselves. Ask students to identify the kinds of movements which best capture the rhythm and the meaning of the poem.

SHOPTALK

Hughes, Langston. *The Book of Rhythms.* New York: Oxford University Press, 1995.

This remarkable children's book was written in 1954, after Mr. Hughes taught interdisciplinary lessons on rhythm at the University of Chicago. The present edition, with an introduction by musician Wynton Marsalis, would be a great addition to your professional library. Illustrations by Matt Wawiorka highlight Mr. Hughes' meditations on rhythm in visual arts, nature, poetry, machines, daily life, and the music and dance of different cultures. Certain topical references are clearly from the 50s, but the inspiring connections to rhythm and Langston Hughes' lyrical writing have timeless value.

Shape

The design concept of shape makes dance movement defined and distinctive. Consider turning your workspace into an art studio where students create living sculptures as they investigate connections to geometry and to concepts such as asymmetry and contrast.

Exploring Shapes

Everything that occupies space in the universe has a shape. Take a moment to look at the space around you. Whether you are sitting outdoors, in your classroom, or in your living room, you are surrounded by things of different shapes. Observe those things with curved shapes. What do you see? A distant hill or mountain? How about in your classroom? Do you see a round wall clock? certain alphabet letters on the wall? Now take a moment to discover the kinds of curved shapes you can make with your fingers and hands. Expand the exploration of curves into your arms.

Look for the straight-lined shapes in your environment. If you are outside in a rural area, you'll notice more curves and fewer straight lines. But spiky, straight leaves poke out of the ground, as do tree trunks, and, of course, human-made structures like a barn. If you are in a city or indoors, you'll notice many straight lines and fewer curves. Except for certain decorations or dramatic,  innovative architecture, most buildings comprise straight-lined shapes. Indoors, wall seams, windows, ceiling panels, doors, bulletin boards, books, tables, and area rugs dominate. See how many straight-lined shapes you can make with your fingers, hands, and arms. Now observe how many things are made out of a combination of curved and straight-lined shapes. Experiment with your fingers, hands, arms, and whole body to make similar shapes.

Geometry

Students can use their knowledge of curved and straight-lined shapes to reinforce their understanding of geometry. The following learning event engages students in exploring circles.

Learning Event

Circle

Introduction. Focus students on what they will be learning.

Suggested music. Something slow and peaceful like *Structures from Silence* by Steve Roach.

Movement exploration. As students sit on their home bases, have them identify objects in the classroom made up of curved lines. Ask them to discover all the different ways they can make different *curved shapes* with their fingers, hands, arms, and whole bodies. During this exploration, students become conscious of curved shapes in their minds, muscles, and imaginations all at the same time.

Circle. Point to the classroom clock or other circular object, and ask students to discover different ways to create this shape with their body parts or whole body. Have them label it a *circle*.

Walk among them and observe their choices.

Sidecoaching. As you walk around, coach students to help them grasp the movement problem with greater clarity and discover more movement possibilities. Rather than telling students exactly what to do or commenting on whether they are successful in solving the movement problem, call out general observations. "I see people making circles with both hands. I see people curving their torsos and arms forward to make circle shapes." Your observations acknowledge the students who are on the right track, and give other students who may be less clear in their movements information that helps them expand their movement choices. As students come closer to solving the problem, they will make choices that are quite unique.

Encourage students to use different levels—standing, sitting, lying down—to find more solutions to the problem. Keep in mind that arms and torsos are better suited than legs to make curved shapes. But you will recognize those who intend to round their legs.

Half-circles. Ask students to cut the circle in half and create half-circle shapes with their body parts and whole body. Walk around and sidecoach as you observe their choices.

Pairs. Pair students up and ask them to discover different circle shapes together. When they first get together they're apt to chatter a bit because making a movement shape together is probably a totally new experience. Exchanging a few words may actually help them make the transition into working this way together. After a minute or so, refocus students by reminding them that they are learning how to communicate through movement, not spoken words.

Aesthetic awareness. As students work by themselves or in pairs, observe whether they are fulfilling the roundness of the shapes in their arms and torsos as they create circles. Very often their elbows or wrists sag which breaks the curved line of the arms. Or, students forget to complete the arc of the torso by including the neck and head in the total shape. Use yourself as a model. Ask students to tell you how you could best fulfill the circle shape with your arms or torso and neck and head. Then ask them to infuse their movements with the same awareness.

Culminating sequence. Ask students to choose three different or favorite ways to make a circle. With younger children, call out a request for each choice. Older children can be given time to select their three shapes. To practice the sequence, cue them to assemble each shape at the sound of a drum beat. Then focus pairs on how they get in and out of each shape by challenging them to form each circle smoothly in four slow drum beats. Ultimately, you want them to move from shape to shape without stopping. Allow students to run through their sequence three times.

Observation. Divide the class into three groups of pairs. Ask each group to demonstrate their circle sequences while the rest of the class watches. What did students see? Ask students to be specific when they talk about their classmates' circles. For example, how did their classmates use size, level, and parts of the body to make circles?

Reflection. While observing and describing movements with words sharpen students' aesthetic perception as well as their verbal skills, consider strengthening your students' spatial intelligence by asking them to draw their impressions of the circle shapes they created and observed.

Students can follow a similar progression while exploring straight-lined shapes and triangles. Have them divide into groups of three to investigate shapes made of three straight lines. Remind them to consider size, level, and whether to use parts of their bodies or whole bodies. Then ask them to create and present their different triangles.

Lettermaking

Primary grades can extend their work in curved and straight-lined shapes by making the letters of the alphabet with their body parts and whole bodies. Focus on meaningful letters—the letters of their name, the letter of the alphabet being highlighted in your classroom, or letters that will eventually build up to simple words like *cold* or *tall* or *wave*. Once students are proficient at making letter shapes, they can get together in small groups to spell out a word with various body shapes. Then they can explore and show the meaning of the word through movement.

SHOPTALK

Yenawine, Philip. *Lines*. New York: Delacorte Press, 1991.

———. *Shapes*. New York: Delacorte Press, 1991.

These wonderful books for children from the Museum of Modern Art, highlight the concepts of line and shape in visual arts. You can use them to offer visual support for students' kinesthetic exploration of shapes and pathways. Both books showcase the work of major artists and provide a rich resource for children who are creating their own dances.

Symmetry and Asymmetry

Students can explore the concepts of symmetry and asymmetry through body shapes. Invite a student to come up to the front of the room to demonstrate. Ask her to stand tall and stretch her arms out to her sides at shoulder level to make a long horizontal line that is parallel to the floor. Ask the rest of the class to imagine that a dotted line is dividing the right and left sides of her body. Point out how the presence of the exact same shape on either side of her body reflects symmetry. Ask her to bend her left arm at the elbow and lift her lower arm to make a vertical line. Point out that the shape the student volunteer is making is now asymmetrical because both sides look different and are no longer identical.

Working in pairs, students can stand shoulder to shoulder so that each person represents the right or left side of a vertical plane. Ask them to imagine that a line runs straight up and down between them. They can stay physically connected—by holding hands or touching identical body parts like shoulders—and create symmetrical shapes. Then they can experience the absence of symmetry by connecting through different body parts and making shapes that aren't identical. Divide the class into two groups and have each group observe the other so everyone can see, as well as feel, the difference between symmetry and asymmetry.

Negative and positive space. Students can explore the concepts of positive and negative space in the visual arts. Positive space refers to the space occupied by images or objects while negative space refers to the empty space that exists around and between objects. Groups of three students can create powerful living sculptures by interconnecting curved and straight-lined shapes. Other students can observe, point out, and draw the positive space—the shapes the students are making with their bodies—and negative space around and between these shapes.

Group Studies of Contrast

Understanding contrast is an essential creative principle in all the arts and in written expression, and is also a key component of critical thinking. Students can create group studies of contrast by synthesizing what they've learned in dance, math, and visual arts. Nowhere is contrast more palpable than in movement and dance. Many of the movement concepts students have already explored not only look different, they feel quite different to the mover.

Task. Students create two *contrasting* group shapes.

Sequence. They begin by standing apart; they come together to create their first group shape.

Next, they break apart and create their second contrasting group shape. They use contrasting movements to get into and out of each shape.

Understanding contrast is an essential creative principle in all the arts and in written expression, and is also a key component of critical thinking.

Field Notes: Teacher-To-Teacher

To enhance students' awareness of design, I show or have them research works by modern painters, such as Klee, Mondrian, Picasso, and sculptors, such as Moore, Noguchi, and Calder which reflect a strong consciousness of curved and/or straight-lined shapes. Sometimes I ask students to observe the work more closely through a "viewfinder"—a one by two-inch rectangle cut out of the middle of a piece of paper. This helps students identify the specific design features of each painting or sculpture, as well as how those parts relate to and comprise a whole.

Diana Cummins
Dance Educator
Los Angeles, California

Guiding the Work

Step out the task together with students. Make sure to include criteria that will help make the group studies more compelling and effective. For example, each group study will

- demonstrate contrast
- have a clear starting and end point
- be repeatable
- use a variety of movements, shapes, and rhythms
- flow without stopping
- be performed with clear energy.

While you give students time to create the first shape, go around and view their work process. Once you see that each group has a shape they can repeat, ask them to create the contrasting shape. Remind them that how they get into each shape must also demonstrate contrast. Then invite them to put the whole sequence together.

You can guide K-2 children to make one group shape within specific parameters such as, "move slowly into a sculpture made of circles." Then ask them to create a completely different group shape. Or suggest that they move quickly into a sculpture made of angled, straight lines. If they have trouble understanding the problem, go back to a movement exploration which contrasts shape, size, energy, and speed so they can feel and see the differences.

Presentation and observation. Let all the groups perform their work. Primary students can discuss the kinds of movements and designs which made each group shape different. Upper elementary students can be guided to observe whether the criteria was fulfilled. Ask students how the group studies could have been made stronger. Inviting observations without naming names engages everyone in critical thinking, but does not put individuals on the spot. After students offer comments, give the groups the opportunity to revise their work and show it again. Ask observers to note any changes and whether or not they were effective.

Pathways

Pathway is most often associated with the path created as the whole body travels through space. It can have different kinds of designs—from straight to curved to zig-zag to circular. For example, if we walked down a narrow, straight sidewalk with paint on the bottom of our shoes, our shoe prints would form a straight pathway.

This spatial concept also refers to body part pathways. In Chapter 4, I used the example, "A child's fingertips trace a curve when her arms swing as she skips." The curve is the pathway created by the girl's fingertips. In the following movement explorations, you'll ask students to explore a new strategy called skywriting. In skywriting, children use different body parts to make pathways in the space around them. Students will then have the opportunity to connect this movement activity to handwriting.

Learning about Skywriting

If you recall the analogy I made in the first chapter between a painter and a dance artist, I mentioned that the space is like a dancer's canvas. I compared the body and parts of the body to brushes of different thicknesses. Students can put this analogy into action when they skywrite.

Movement exploration. Ask students to imagine they have a floor-to-ceiling canvas in front of them. They also have a big, thick paintbrush in their hand, and a bucket of paint sitting on the floor below the canvas. Everyone dips into their buckets and starts painting continuous curved lines on the canvas in front of them.

Sidecoaching. As students explore curving pathways in the space around them, give students new directions that will allow them to vary the kinds of continuous lines they are drawing, without stopping the flow of movement. This form of coaching is an invaluable facilitation tool. Student's use their kinesthetic intelligence to make connections through movements that build on each other. Staying in motion also keeps students highly focused.

Coach students to integrate their knowledge of different movement concepts to vary their movements. Ask them to paint curved lines that go from very *low* to very *high* on the canvas. Inscribe these swirling and curling lines with different *speeds*. Dab very *tiny* lines, stroke very *large* lines. Students can experiment using *strong* and *weak* energy to inscribe these looping, wavy lines.

To make movements more full-bodied and increase the versatility of other body parts, ask students to dip the paintbrush into the bucket once again, then imagine the brush is taped to their elbow. You'll see that when students use other body parts, they discover different kinds of movements. Take a moment to experience the difference yourself.

Have students imagine the canvas now surrounds their home base, as if they are standing in a large, spacious cylinder. Ask them to inscribe lines of different sizes, heights, speeds, and energy with one shoulder and then the other, as they turn around at their homebase. Ask them to place the paintbrush on one knee, then the other. What happens? They are standing on one leg balancing as the other knee inscribes curved lines in front of them. Have them put the paintbrush on their toes. What happens? Does anyone paint the ceiling?

Skywriting and handwriting. To help children make the transition from creating curved pathways to handwriting, it's important to supply a writing implement that's stiffer than a brush, one which will feel similar to a pencil or pen. Ask students to exchange their paintbrushes for a thick piece of chalk. Primary students can explore straight and curved lines that make up print lettering, while older students can experience and identify the components of cursive handwriting—under curves, over curves, loops, and circles. Start by asking students to write their full names. Once they are fully focused on the task, challenge them to make their signatures bigger, smaller, higher, lower, faster, and slower, without losing fullness and accuracy.

A wonderful exercise is to have students create their own "movement signatures" by infusing their movements with their own special brand of

Field Notes: Teacher-To-Teacher

While my third graders were studying the Cheyenne, they selected Native American names for themselves such as Wandering Dog, Calming Waters, and Soaring Eagle, and created shields to symbolically depict their names. Next, they worked with a partner to create a dance sequence. Students revealed their name through movement, as if they were introducing themselves to one another.

Pam Strain
Emma W. Shuey Elementary School
Rosemead, California

buoyant, quiet, easygoing, or intense energy. If there's room, let students move across the space as if inscribing their names on a giant chalkboard.

Traveling Freely in the Space

Tell students you are going to invite them to travel through the space in a special, new way. It will demand the utmost of them as responsible movers. You're going to cue them to start walking anywhere they want to in the space. While they are traveling, they must listen carefully for a freeze signal and for directions that will ask them to move in different ways. Remind them that all the same agreements about spatial awareness apply: they need to watch where they're going to avoid bumping or talking to anyone.

Cue students to start walking anywhere they want to in the space. Since this is a new strategy, it is very useful to give them *a point of focus*. Like going somewhere with a sense of purpose, students will feel confident knowing *how* they are supposed to move. Also, you want to test their ability to carry out a new set of directions without stopping the flow of movement. Choose a simple command.

"Make your steps small."
Students comply and keep taking small steps until they hear the next set of directions from you.

"Make your steps big and light."
Keep integrating different movement concepts until you can see everyone understands this new spatial strategy. Then play the freeze signal. Students should stop in their tracks and freeze their whole body in active stillness.

Let's summarize the steps of moving freely in the space.

- You set students into motion with a sound cue. They travel wherever they want to in the space.
- You give directions to change how they are moving; they maintain those changes until they hear the next set of directions.
- Using a sound cue, you stop students for a momentary rest or to hear directions which need their full attention.

Curved Pathways

A buoyant piece of music, such as the title track from *Mountain Light* by Rob Whitesides-Woo, works well with this exploration.

Movement exploration. Ask students to walk freely in space while stepping easily to the beat of the music. Direct their attention to the pathways they are making. Most will already be walking in curved pathways. Ask them to exaggerate the curved pathways they are traveling on as they walk in and around each other.

Once students grasp this spatial strategy, ask them to change how they are traveling, yet remain on curved pathways. Encourage them to explore steps of different sizes, levels, and energies. For those of you who are working with K-2 children, remember to call out the changes as they travel.

Cause and Effect in Nature

Creative movement offers a way to explore cause and effect in nature. Students can show what they know about the relationship between natural forces such as the influence of wind on the landscape.

If possible, have students stand outdoors so they can experience a breeze or gust of wind. Ask them to observe how the wind moves natural objects such as tree branches or grass, and human-made objects like flags or awnings.

Back in the classroom, ask students to explore the motion of wind by moving like a gentle breeze on curved pathways in the workspace. They can increase their speed gradually and intensify their energy, from weak to strong, as they travel. Guide them to explore different levels, and bursts of strong energy like gusts. Direct them to slow down gradually until the air is still. Talk them through the sequence, then let them present the whole movement sequence on their own.

Creative movement offers a way to explore cause and effect in nature.

Primary. Divide the children into two groups. One group can take the shape of vegetation—tall trees with long branches, thick clumps of bushes, beds of flowers. The other group can move like the wind in and around the bushes, trees, and flowers, and so on. Students who are representing vegetation can show the impact of the wind through swaying, shivering, and bending motions.

Upper. Older children can create group studies based on the relationship between wind and earth erosion. Remind students who are exploring the

Field Notes: Teacher-To-Teacher

While working on a science unit called "Project I'M ME" (Inventors, Mathematics, Motion, and Energy) it was natural for our students to express what they learned by using the elements of dance. Each group's research and area of expertise led them to connect their learning with movement and dance that illustrated Newton's Laws of Motion, forces, friction, or gravity. It was amazing to see the relationship between these concepts and the elements of dance. Most memorable were the human roller coaster our students created to demonstrate velocity and acceleration, and their use of the earth ball to show Newton's Law of Inertia.

Char Girard and Richard Jacobsen
Emma W. Shuey School
Rosemead, California

actions of the wind to integrate strong and weak energy as they explore different pathways and velocities. Students exploring landforms can create distinctive shapes that change in response to the wind-like actions of their classmates.

Straight Pathways

Every time we travel from one point directly to another—from a kitchen chair to the sink or down a long school corridor—we move on a straight pathway. Straight pathways can also consist of interconnecting straight lines which make right angles. Imagine a city neighborhood arranged in rectangular blocks. Visualize your pathway if you travel three blocks north, two blocks east, and one block south. Straight pathways can also be created from interconnecting diagonal lines known as zig-zags.

Changing directions. When the whole body changes direction, it turns. Changes in directions while traveling in curved pathways appear seamless. The body simply turns in arcs of continuous motion. The challenge of traveling on a pathway of interconnecting straight lines is that the body has to turn, or pivot, very precisely. Think of soldiers during a changing of the guard. They take a few steps, pivot crisply again on the balls of their feet, take another few steps, pivot again and stand at full attention. To introduce students to moving in straight pathways, it's helpful, first, to acquaint them with changing directions in precise ways.

Body facings. Stand in the front of the room and ask your students to face you squarely as they would in a warm-up. Tell them you are going to call out a command and cue them with a sharp drum beat to face different walls in the room as quickly and precisely as they can.

Cue them to face the back wall. Students will either pivot on their feet or take a tiny jump to make the half turn. Next, cue them to return to face the front wall. Ask students to point to their right, then face the "right side wall," a quarter turn. Have them return to facing front. Ask them to point to, then face the "left side wall." Have them experience a quarter turn while facing one of the side walls so they face the back wall. Once they are fully acquainted with each direction, challenge your students by giving commands quickly and asking them to face the walls in random order.

Traveling on Straight Pathways

Younger children can move off, then return to their home base on straight pathways that travel forward, backward, and sideways. See what happens if they take four steps forward, then four steps away from each of the walls, while facing the walls with the front of their bodies. (They will travel forward then backward then pivot a quarter turn to travel in each new direction.) Try this yourself. What happens if they travel four steps toward, then four steps away from each of the four walls, but have to keep their body facing the front wall the whole time? Try this yourself.

Challenge students to travel off then back to their home base propelled by different facings of their bodies. See what happens if students let specific parts of their bodies, such as their elbows, lead them in these different directions. They can also vary their movements by changing the types, sizes, levels, and energies of their steps.

Invite older students to travel freely in the space to explore straight pathways. First, ask them to walk on pathways that make right angles. They can maintain the precision of their directions by facing one of the four walls squarely at all times. Once you see they have grasped the movement problem and are highly focused while traveling forward, challenge them to move their bodies sideways and backwards, as they move in straight-lined pathways. Remind them to focus carefully in these new directions so they don't bump into anyone.

You can use whole turns, half-turns, and quarter turns—even one-eighth turns when students pivot halfway between the front and side walls—to help students understand and show what they know about fractions. Students can also step out angles and geometric shapes on the floor.

Mapping a Journey

Maps of specific areas—a local neighborhood, a city, a stretch of countryside, a state, a country, the world—record and reflect a wealth of information through their visual designs and symbols. The following strategies, based on using maps in the classroom, can help students understand what maps tell us about an area, as well as how they guide our travel through areas that may be new to us.

Maps for the primary grades. Sketch a map of your classroom from a bird's-eye perspective. Choose three areas or pieces of furniture that can serve as landmarks. Choose a pathway that starts from the first landmark—the starting point—and proceeds to the second landmark. Chart a second pathway from the second landmark to the third landmark. Create a final pathway from the third landmark back to the first one. Try to include pathways that are curved as well as straight.

Since you are going to direct small groups of students to travel, decide how they should move. At this point, you and your students know various traveling movements—walks, runs, jumps, hops, and skips, as well as movement concepts to draw upon—size, level, speed, weight, and force. Keep your choices simple, but be sure to provide a sense of contrast. For example, students can skip lightly from the reading corner to your desk. From your desk to the learning center, they can creep in low, sideways walks. From the learning center back to the reading corner, they can run on a curved path, then freeze in a big shape.

To inspire your students into action, point out the landmarks, describe the movement tasks of each pathway verbally, then have a small group demonstrate. Each group that follows can respond to your verbal directions for each leg of the journey. Then challenge each group to complete the whole journey without any verbal prompting from you.

With first and second grades, draw a bigger version of the map you sketched of the classroom on the chalkboard. Explain that you are going to use this map to write down and remember where they traveled and what kinds of movements they did. You can either inscribe the pathways on the map yourself, or have student volunteers come up and draw them. Invite students to make symbols for the traveling movements they used.

Map extension. As students become acquainted with maps and understand the relationship between the classroom space and the sketch you shared with them on the chalkboard, you can make copies of your map on paper. Divide students into collaborative learning groups and give each group a map. Ask students to draw different pathways, choose different ways to travel, and create different symbols for their maps. Next, invite them to get up and put their maps into action.

Maps for upper grades. Divide students into groups of five. Have each group explore the classroom as if encountering it on a geographical expedition for the first time. Ask them to note the sizes, levels, and shapes of the furniture and objects in the room, as well as the distances between these "landmarks." Then have them select three major landmarks.

Ask each group to create a map of the classroom which reflects the location of major landmarks as well as any empty space they can travel through. Students can apply what they know about *perspective* and *scale* by drawing classroom furniture and empty space in correct proportions.

Each group can choose three routes through the classroom to and from three different landmarks. Pathways should be straight or curved, or can be a combination of both. Then have the groups decide how to move on each pathway. Offer a list of locomotor movements as well as movement concepts they already know. Have them design symbols for how to move along each pathway. They can refer to the key of an existing map for help.

Invite the whole class to get up and practice putting their maps into action. Point out they need to be extra careful while moving so students don't bump into classmates who are also practicing. If the classroom is too crowded, you can have a few groups go at one time. Give students the chance to revise their pathways and movement choices; they may have found a more interesting pathway or way to move while they were in action. If they make changes, give them time to change their maps.

Now students can put their maps into action one group at a time. Have each group memorize the pathways and movements encoded on their maps so they can move as freely as possible from landmark to landmark. Have the other students observe and describe the kinds of pathways and traveling movements they see. After a group has put their map into action, pass around their map so classmates can see the pathways and symbols the group created.

To emphasize how maps guide others into unknown territory through visual symbols, you can have the groups exchange maps and put them into action. Give all the groups time to figure out the directions of the new map they've been given. Then ask one group at a time to show how each map guides them through the space.

Observation. Once again, students will witness the unique movement invention of their classmates. Even though a group is following the same directions as the one which created the original map, exactly how the maps are decoded will vary. Ask students to articulate the differences they see in each group's movement choices.

Geography Journey

The classroom can be used to represent any geographical area—the school neighborhood, your town, the ocean, the mountains, a forest, the sky, your state, the United States, the world. If you and your students are feeling creative and adventurous, you can rearrange furniture so that you recreate neighborhoods, forge trails through forests, or create an ocean habitat.

How students move is influenced by what kind of terrain and natural barriers they enact or encounter as travelers in each place. For example, ask your students to identify the kinds of movement knowledge they can draw upon to understand how a river journeys from the mountains to the sea:

- size—How wide and deep is the river at its source? Does the river cascade down a mountainside? meander through a meadow? spill out into the sea?
- level—What elevations does the river travel through from the mountains to the sea?
- shape—What is the shape of the land forms the river impacts?
- pathways—What is the design of the river's pathway in the mountains? through meadows? through cities? as it spills out to sea?
- strong and weak energy—How does the river flow at different elevations? How does the volume of water affect the intensity of its flow?
- acceleration and deceleration—How quickly or slowly does the river flow at different elevations? in different pathways?

Discuss with your class a geography journey through the natural world they can plan, map out, and put into action in your classroom. They can synthesize their learning in social studies, dance, science, and literature to create this journey. Remember—they need to choose movements and sequences which capture the essence of the journey, not enact it literally.

Portrait of a Knowledgeable, Creative Mover

Let's look, as we have in previous chapters, at how we might assess the work of a mid-elementary student.

Participation. The student is able to work on his or her own, with a partner, in a trio, or in a group as a collaborative problem-solver. The student understands and is able to fulfill the demands of the creative process: exploring, making movement choices, sequencing, and presenting.

Movement. The student is able to draw on his or her knowledge of the elements of dance to explore movement problems; can combine different movement concepts simultaneously; can generate original movements; can create rhythmic patterns; can sequence varied movements into a seamless whole.

Aesthetic awareness. As *a mover*: the student can articulate his or her understanding of shape, size, level, pathway, force, weight, quality, speed, and rhythm with body parts and whole body—in place and through space; the student can help formulate criteria to make classwork as compelling and effective as possible. *As an observer*: the student can label and describe the movements classmates use to create group studies; can assess whether criteria have been met; and can evaluate the effectiveness of his or her classmates' group studies.

As students become knowledgeable about the elements of dance, they explore, synthesize, and demonstrate knowledge in meaningful and defined ways.

Field Notes: Teacher-To-Teacher

Judy Singleton's kindergarten students were reading "A River Runs Wild" in their Great American Stories Unit, and working with movement and dance in their study of the river. Students explored the concept of water flowing in one direction only, by running with scarves from one end of the classroom to the other and then walking along the sides of the room back to the other side. Levels varied as the river got deep and shallow. Some students danced the part of water and some curled up on the floor to simulate pebbles. As students passed over them with scarves, the pebbles rolled with the current. In an advanced class several days later, they used the scarves between one another to form a circle with three to four students in each group. Each student held one end of the scarf as they formed eddies in the river. Then the class discussed how eddies affect the current, leading them to talk about water safety. After one week of working with these movements, Singleton's students created a river dance set to cello music for their final performance.

Jean Miller McComb
Movement Curriculum Consultant
Hannah McClure Elementary School
Winchester, Kentucky

Curriculum content. The student demonstrates knowledge of concepts such as cause and effect in nature through sequences of expressive, detailed movements; the student is able to synthesize learning in several disciplines, such as visual arts, math, and dance, to express understanding with clarity and depth; the student is able to reflect orally, in writing, and through drawing.

As you absorb this portrait, think back to the beginning of the movement and dance process. In the natural movement phase, you asked students to engage in ordinary movements. Look at how your students have progressed. As students have experienced warm-ups and movement explorations, they've become acquainted with the versatility of their bodies as expressive instruments and have become knowledgeable about the elements of dance. As a result, they can explore, synthesize, and demonstrate knowledge in meaningful and defined ways.

Chapter 6

How To Design Your Own Lessons

All teaching begins by deciding what students are ready to learn and are interested in, and selecting appropriate content and strategies. It's clear that movement and dance can provide stimulating ways for students to learn and express themselves. You might ask, then, when is it appropriate to integrate movement and dance into my instruction?

One way to determine if your students should experience movement and dance is to ask yourself questions as you focus on specific curriculum areas:

- What topics, concepts, or processes can be explored and illuminated through movement and dance?
- How can students investigate and communicate what they are learning through movement?

Selecting Content and Strategies

Let's answer these questions together. We'll use the water cycle as an example of how to build meaningful movement and dance experiences for your students.

What topics, concepts, or processes can be illuminated? First, you need to identify the "movement potential" of a curriculum area. Ask yourself if this area contains any motion or distinctive shapes that students can explore as movers. Since water molecules rise up, collect together, and fall back down to earth, it's clear the water cycle can be investigated through movement.

What can students learn? The water cycle is composed of three underlying processes: evaporation, cloud formation, and precipitation. Evaporation is an invisible process students can understand more deeply through motion. They can relate to water molecules by experiencing heavy energy while lying on the ground. They can understand how water molecules are transformed by the heat of the sun by experiencing the quality and path of those heated molecules through movement that rises and is filled with light energy. By creating cloud shapes, students can learn how water droplets cluster together to form clouds. Exploring movements which fall from high to low levels can help students understand how water drops out of clouds as rain.

Students can also grasp abstract concepts embedded in the water cycle through motion. For example, students can

- comprehend the nature of a cycle by experiencing, then repeating the whole process
- reinforce the concept of cause and effect by exploring how water molecules rise up, collect together, and fall back down because they are at the effect of other forces such as the sun, cooler air, and gravity
- understand the theme of change by focusing on how the water molecules are transformed.

Experiencing cycle, cause and effect, and transformation through motion anchors students' understanding of these concepts in their bodies, minds, and imaginations.

Planning the Learning Experience

Once you have decided the water cycle is worth exploring through movement, you need to make some decisions regarding your workspace. The limitations of the space will affect the design and progression of your lessons. Will students move in available classroom space? a cleared classroom? a multi-purpose room?

Planning and facilitation tools. The Movement and Dance Lesson Framework summarizes the key components of the learning events modeled in this book. Whatever your objective, you'll be able to plan a meaningful learning experience for your students as you follow this progression.

Movement and Dance Lesson Framework

Objective. You and students envision what and how to learn.

Focus. Students explore what they already know; establish personal space.

Warm-up. Students prepare to move in defined, expressive ways.

Movement exploration. Students learn through problem solving.

Curriculum connection. Students deepen, extend, and demonstrate learning in other curriculum areas.

Culminating sequence. Students communicate learning by constructing and presenting a sequence or group study.

Observation and assessment. Students watch to learn; you and students assess.

Cool-down and reflection. Students refocus energy; you and students reflect on what was learned and what to learn next.

Students can reinforce understanding, make connections across disciplines, and communicate their learning through dance.

You can use the Dance Resource Chart on page 110, created by movement specialist and educator W. Rex Comer, as a planning tool to help choose the content of your movement and dance lessons. You can also use it as a facilitation tool to vary the movements students are exploring while conducting a learning event. Students can use the chart as a creative resource while constructing sequences, group studies, and dances. In the next chapter, you'll see how you and your students can use the Dance Resource Chart as a tool to understand the aesthetic choices dance artists make to communicate their visions. Consider enlarging, laminating, and posting it in your classroom for easy reference.

Determining your objectives. To establish your objectives for working with the water cycle, consider what you want students to learn. Will they be reinforcing their understanding of single topics, concepts, and processes? connecting their learning to disciplines besides dance and science? synthesizing and communicating their learning through a creative movement study?

Let's say students will

- deepen their understanding of the water cycle by exploring evaporation, cloud formation, rain, and puddles through movement
- connect their learning in dance and science to poetry
- synthesize their learning by creating and presenting a group study that communicates what they know and feel about storms.

Dance Resource Chart

Instrument

Whole Body and Body Parts

Head • Shoulders • Elbows • Arms
Hands • Torso • Hips • Legs • Feet

Movement

Movement in Place (axial)
Shake • Gesture • Stretch • Contract • Bend • Turn • Twist • Balance

Movement through Space (locomotor)
Crawl • Roll • Walk • Run • Leap • Jump • Hop • Skip • Gallop • Slide

The Elements of Dance

Space	Energy	Time
Size	**Force**	**Speed**
Big	Strong	Slow
Small	Weak	Fast
		Acceleration
Level	**Weight**	Deceleration
High	Heavy	
Medium	Light	**Rhythm**
Low		Natural Time
	Quality	Steady Beat
Shape	Smooth	
Curved	Sharp	
Straight	Swing	
Directions	**Stillness**	
Forward	Active	
Backward	Passive	
Sideways		
Diagonal		
Pathway		
Straight		
Curved		
Circular		
Zig-Zag		
Relationships		
Near		
Apart		

Keep in mind that younger children will need to experience the key components of the water cycle in simpler ways than older students. For them, exploring the contrast between evaporation and cloud formation will be plenty for one lesson. Then you can engage them in another lesson to conclude their exploration of the whole cycle (rain and puddles). Older students can explore evaporation, cloud formation, and rain and puddle formation in one learning experience.

As you plan your lesson, you'll want to

- identify movement possibilities within each part of the water cycle
- select movement concepts from the Dance Resource Chart for your students to explore
- sketch out a culminating sequence, then plan backward to design the warm-up, movement exploration, and curriculum connection.

DIALOGUE

Envision what evaporation, cloud formation, rain, and puddles look like and how they move. Then use your Dance Resource Chart to relate those actions and descriptors to the movement concepts embedded in Space, Energy, and Time. How does water vapor move? What are the sizes and shapes of clouds, rain, and puddles? What kinds of energies are at work as water molecules move and change? What kinds of speeds are involved in each part of the process?

_____

_____

_____

You probably thought of movement concepts such as the following.

Water Cycle	Space	Energy	Time
evaporation (rising)	low to high level	light energy	slow speed
cloud formation (drifting)	large, curved shapes moving across space	light to heavy energy	slow speed
rain (falling)	high to low level small movements	heavy energy	quick speed
puddles (lying on ground)	low level curved shapes	passive stillness	

Creating a Culminating Sequence

Once you have identified the key actions and movement concepts for your students to explore, sketch out a culminating sequence that will help them coalesce what they're learning and demonstrate what they know. Previous learning events model a variety of culminating sequences you can revisit and build upon, depending on the curriculum area you are working with.

The water cycle offers you the opportunity to work with an embedded sequence. Students can connect to its beginning—evaporation—and simply follow its natural progression to the formation of puddles. Remember to assign a certain number of beats to each part of the cycle so students know how long their movements should last. Decide, also, if students are to fulfill the sequence by themselves, in pairs, or in small groups.

DIALOGUE

Describe your culminating sequence in simple sentences.

_____

_____

_____

_____

The Movement and Dance Lesson Framework

After you've designed your culminating sequence, planning the rest of the learning experience becomes clear-cut. Simply ask yourself what your students need to know and do to fulfill the demands of the culminating sequence. This is your guiding question as you design the warm-up, movement exploration, and curriculum connection.

Focusing students. To focus students on the topics as well as their movement potentials, ask them to help you web weather and clouds. Then focus specifically on rain. Ask older students to be specific about the different kinds of clouds and to identify those clouds which are rain clouds. In telling you how clouds and rain are formed, ask students to comment on how clouds and rain move.

The warm-up. Remember that a warm-up is essential to prepare students' whole bodies and body parts for moving. You can use the warm-ups we've tried in previous chapters or adapt your own warm-up to include movement concepts involved in the day's lesson.

Movement exploration. The movement exploration serves to acquaint students with the main movement concepts they will be using to connect to the curriculum area. This is the time to access students' knowledge of particular movement concepts central to the day's lesson, such as heavy and light energy, and curved shapes.

So you've decided on the content of the exploration. Now you need to choose the spatial strategy that will best support your students' investigation of those movement concepts. Students can work

- in place
- off, then back to their home bases
- as they travel freely through space
- with partners
- in small groups.

Again, envisioning the processes underlying the water cycle will help you make the most appropriate selections. You might decide to have students explore light rising movements and heavier falling movements in place. As demonstrated in previous learning events, students can put different movement energies into their body parts and then into their whole bodies.

Curriculum connection. There are several ways to invite students to integrate their movement and dance knowledge with the curriculum topic. Ask students to

- recall what they know about the water cycle, then ask them to move as if they are water evaporating, clouds forming, and rain falling
- read about and look at illustrations, photographs, and a video related to the water cycle, then investigate how this subject or process moves.

The movement exploration acquaints students with the movement concepts they'll use to connect to the curriculum area.

Once children make the curriculum connection, plan to let them investigate it on their own, especially if they are working with partners or in small groups. You can ask them to explore the separate parts of the culminating sequence. For example, students can spend a few minutes finding different ways to rise up from the floor in light, smooth movements like water vapor. Then you can ask them to assemble in small clusters to find different ways to make round, billowing clouds. Students can then practice traveling across the space while making a big, soft curved shape like a cloud.

Culminating sequence. Since you have already designed the culminating sequence, just plan how to introduce it to your students. To start, you can talk younger students through it, then cue their actions with different sound sources. Older students can follow written directions and put the whole sequence into motion. Be sure to establish criteria with students describing the movement task and how it should be fulfilled.

Movement curriculum consultant Jean Miller McComb suggests supporting students' movements with a rain stick—a hollowed out branch that is filled with seeds, which makes a sound similar to cascading rain drops when it's tipped. You can also use recordings of rainstorms.

Field Notes: Teacher-To-Teacher

To show my students how water collects in clouds and becomes rain, I soak a sponge in a pie pan filled with water. Then I ask one of my students to lift the sponge up over the pan to demonstrate how the sponge (acting as a cloud) cannot hold any more water, so water (the rain) drips down from it. This demonstration helps children understand heaviness, gravity, and why rain falls from clouds.

Nancy Gates
Savannah Elementary School
Rosemead, California

Aesthetic awareness. Once again, it's important to point out that students are not engaged in literal movements that mime the water cycle. They will explore and communicate the essence of evaporation, condensation, and precipitation. They'll draw upon their knowledge of level, size, weight, force, shape, and speed to discover distinctive movements. Each student will invent their own way to rise up with light energy, make large, soft, round shapes, and express staccato drips of rain. The essence of rain may appear in one child's shaking shoulders or another's quickly tapping feet. You won't know until your students' choices appear, newly discovered, right before your eyes.

Observation and assessment. You want enough students to show their work at the same time so they feel comfortable. As always, ask students to share what was communicated by their classmates' movement sequences, and how this information was expressed. Ask if they learned anything new or surprising about the water cycle, or if they were struck by a particularly effective way a classmate expressed his or her understanding. Did students follow the criteria for the culminating sequence?

Cool-down. Students can relax totally by letting all energy and tension drain out of their bodies. If the floor is clean, plan to let them lie on the floor—in their puddle shapes—with their eyes closed. If you prefer, let them lean forward at their tables and desks and rest their heads on their hands.

Reflection. As you know from past learning events, students can respond orally, through writing, or through drawing to reflect on what they have learned. Your job is to formulate the questions or guidelines to which they respond. Older children can articulate the kinds of connections that exist between their movements and the curriculum area they were investigating by responding to questions such as, "Why did you move with light energy to explore evaporation?" Remember to plan reflection time for yourself. Assessing how the lesson went in your dance journal will strengthen your skills as a guide and help show you where to go next with your class.

Implementing the Lesson

The continuity of a movement and dance learning experience depends on an uninterrupted flow of energy.

Of course, a successful lesson begins with planning ahead. The vitality and sense of continuity of a movement and dance learning experience depend on an uninterrupted flow of energy, and a high level of concentration from your students. If guiding a whole lesson feels overwhelming to you, then implement smaller sections over the course of several days. For example, a warm-up is invigorating and focusing for students. The next day, engage students in a brief warm-up and the movement exploration. The following day, review the warm-up and the exploration, then focus students on the curriculum connection—including the culminating sequence. But remember, the more you involve students in complete lessons, the more practiced they will become in accessing movements and putting them together in creative and meaningful ways.

Besides planning, organizing your support materials is also important. Have your drum and other percussion instruments handy, as well as your cassette recorder, tapes you'll be using, and your visual aids. Posting the steps involved in your lesson will also be helpful.

Facilitation Tips

When presenting a movement problem, clear, succinct commands are the key to success. Once you decide on the task you want students to explore, you need to find the words that invite them to do it. If you come across stumbling blocks along the way, see a list of solutions you may find helpful on page 117.

It's a good idea to let students construct or learn sequences in stages. Let them investigate and repeat the separate parts of sequences before putting them together. After practicing, they can repeat the whole sequence several times without stopping. This will deepen students' understanding of the movement concepts they're exploring and give them the satisfaction of expressing and refining specific choices.

Troubleshooting

Problems	*Solutions*
Students have difficulty grasping the problem.	Stop and ask questions to help them clarify directions.
Students need to vary movements.	Sidecoach to suggest possible choices and movement concepts.
Students have trouble sequencing movements.	Focus on "transitions" so movement ideas can flow together.
Students aren't getting the curriculum connection.	Stop and ask questions.
Students are having difficulty working with each other.	Have groups go over their ground rules for working together.

Thinking on Your Feet

We've all had experiences where we've planned a lesson that doesn't unfold in ways we expected. Flexibility and adaptability are essential, especially when working with movement. Here are some ways to problem solve on your feet in the middle of a lesson, if what you've planned doesn't seem to be working. Ask yourself questions such as the following:

- Do students need to explore movements that are more simple and concrete? more physically demanding? Consult your Dance Resource Chart and see if another concept helps. If that doesn't work, simply switch gears. Engage students on the spot in a strategy from a past lesson, bring it to a conclusion, then analyze what may have gone wrong with your material later on. By simply making another choice for your students to explore, you are keeping the movement experience positive and you are not stopping on a negative note.

- Have I given students enough time to understand the movement problem or curriculum connection? If the answer is no, simply back up. Take them through the steps again so that the movement concepts they need to access are fully developed in their bodies.

- In the excitement of working with movement and dance, have I dropped an essential stitch? Sometimes we leap-frog over an important step in the lesson. Simply back up and keep going.

- Even though the students have achieved the overall objective, am I looking for perfection? Remember, learning about movement happens in its own time. The body is slower than the mind. It takes many visits to really absorb movement concepts. If students aren't fulfilling every step of the lesson fully, move on to the next one, and revisit what was problematic in another lesson.

- Is there something I didn't plan for that is begging to be explored? The first rule of creativity is that surprising new ideas arise in the process itself. No amount of planning can generate moments of true inspiration. Since working with movement and dance is a creative process, it's important for you to give yourself permission to follow through on the unexpected if some exciting movement idea or curriculum connection suddenly presents itself. An open response to the unexpected may lead to exciting new areas of investigation. Furthermore, as you model receptivity for your students, it emboldens them as explorers, problem solvers, and creators.

Integrating More Than One Discipline

If you seek to integrate more than one discipline in movement and dance experiences, begin by deciding how to get into and out of each curriculum area. For example, if you wanted to develop a series of lessons culminating in the exploration of rainstorms, students can

- access their scientific knowledge of weather
- explore aspects of weather through movement
- proceed into language arts to work with poetry (primary) or write a poem (upper)
- go back into movement and dance to put the poetry into motion.

Connecting to Poetry

Let's assume you've lead your primary-grade students through the whole water cycle. They can work with poetry that focuses on rainstorms like selected text from *Water Dance* by Thomas Locker. You can design a movement exploration that reinforces students' understanding of the poetry. Write the selected text or poem on the chalkboard for everyone to see, and read it aloud a few times. Encourage students to respond to the images of the poetry through movement, and integrate what they know about the water cycle. Then ask them to put their understanding of the poetry into motion. Cue them to begin and ask them to freeze in their last shape to show you they've finished. You might consider playing classical selections from *Baroque Guitar* by Julian Bream.

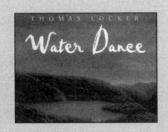

SHOPTALK

Locker, Thomas. *Water Dance.* San Diego: Harcourt Brace, 1997.

Children of all ages will respond to Locker's eloquent images of water as it dances through life on our planet. His poetic text and illustrations capture the motion of rivers, lakes, the ocean, water vapor, clouds, storm fronts, and rain. In the back of the book, Candace Christiansen provides scientific information about the processes underlying the water cycle. This book will help you construct learning experiences that integrate dance, literature, science, and visual arts.

Cinquains. Dance movement specialists Susan Cambigue-Tracey and W. Rex Comer introduced me to a strategy in which upper elementary students write their own *cinquain*—a Japanese form of poetry—and create movement poems based on what they have written.

A cinquain is made up of five lines

Noun

Adjective Adjective
(which modify noun)

Gerund   Gerund   Gerund
(action words related to noun)

a four-word phrase
(describing the actions of the noun)

Synonym

Have students divide into groups of four or five. As they write their cinquains, urge them to think about words related to a storm which are filled with different kinds of motion, shapes, energy, and speeds. This way, students look at storms through a movement "lens," sharpening their language skills. Here's ten-year-old Devora Kaye's interpretation.

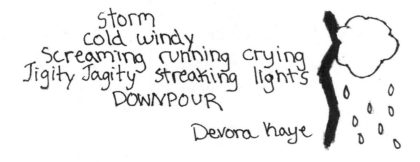

Storm
cold windy
screaming running crying
Jigity Jagity streaking lights
DOWNPOUR

Devora Kaye

Performers realize that audiences seek a compelling experience that only full-bodied, expressive communication can provide.

Planning group strategy. Before asking each group to put their poem into motion, direct them to choose an effective group strategy. Will they all move at the same time to enact the poem? Or will they move all at once some of the time, and divide movement tasks among themselves at other times?

Music and sound sources. Will they have a narrator read the poem aloud as they are moving or recite the poem while they move? Another option is for students to use sound sources—like music or recordings of rain—to support their movement poem, then read their cinquain after.

Movement exploration. Once they make these fundamental decisions, ask students to explore the cinquain through movement. Be sure to have the Dance Resource Chart handy for reference to help them put their poems into action. Encourage them, also, to respond to the poem with their imaginations to communicate the dynamic nature of a storm.

Criteria. Once again, invite students to join with you in developing some criteria for their poetry in motion.

The working process. As students work, walk around and observe each group's process. Students should be moving as they explore the imagery of their poems. They can stop to make decisions and brainstorm on where to go next.

Plan a fifteen-minute working period, then approach each group and tell them you'd like to see what they've sketched so far. This gives students an opportunity to put all their choices together and communicate their movement poem to an audience (of one) for the first time. If they've finished "sketching" their poem through movement, ask them how it felt. Have they accomplished what they set out to do? Is there anything they'd like to change? If you see that they are not meeting some of the criteria, share your observations with the group and urge them to make appropriate revisions. If the group hasn't finished putting the whole poem into action, encourage them to finish, then return after giving feedback to the other groups. After another ten minutes or so, alert the groups that they have five minutes to rehearse before everyone presents their movement poems.

The presentation. Since students first began working with movement in Chapter 3, they have viewed and learned from each other's work. Susan Cambigue-Tracey uses two questions to focus performers and observers:

- As performers, what do you most want from the audience?
- As an audience, what do you most want from the performers?

These viewing guidelines make students think about the process underlying each other's experience. Audience members get to understand that performers need attention and quiet to concentrate properly. Performers realize that audiences seek a compelling experience that only full-bodied, expressive communication can provide.

Suggest to students that along with observing action words associated with storms, they keep their eyes and ears out for the unique ways in which groups have characterized storms in their movement and written poems. Then ask each group to share their movement study.

Ask the audience what they saw. Encourage students to respond to the whole presentation. How did dance poems make them feel? What did the poems make them think about?

Keep in mind that sometimes a group's work gets obscured or falls apart because of performance nerves or missed cues. Perhaps the group needs to focus its attention before they begin their presentation. Whatever the cause, invite the group to clear up the problems they encountered and have another go. It's important for all students to experience a sense of support and safety as they work with processes that are new and require risk-taking.

Field Notes: Teacher-To-Teacher

I invite students to make specific suggestions about how classmates can make their dance poems more compelling by integrating changes in direction, level, size, shape, energy, and rhythm. Specific suggestions help performers revise and refine their work.

Jean Miller McComb
Movement Curriculum Consultant
Frankfort, Kentucky

Revision. Be sure to give all groups the opportunity to absorb their classmates' responses, and to rework their dance poems. Presenting and viewing their work again allows students to see the positive influence of feedback and to connect more deeply to effective, creative strategies.

SHOPTALK

Grant, Janet Millar. *Shake, Rattle, and Learn: Classroom-tested Ideas That Use Movement for Active Learning.* York, Maine: Stenhouse Publishers, 1995; Markham, Ontario: Pembroke Publishers, 1995.

This book offers a wealth of content ideas for movement experiences. Written from the perspective of a classroom teacher, it discusses working with movement across the curriculum. Chapters focus on stories, the environment, interpersonal relationships, body communication, poetry, rhythm, visual design, spatial relationships, and societal issues. Throughout, Grant suggests excellent children's literature as a resource, as well as solid interdisciplinary connections. She and I offer similar strategies, although I focus more on how to facilitate movement experiences and infuse curriculum connections with the elements of dance—which will help you put Grant's rich ideas into action in your classroom.

DIALOGUE

What area of the curriculum can my students explore through movement?

_____

_____

What do I want students to learn? What do they already know?

_____

_____

What do students need to know in movement and dance to make the curriculum connection? Will they integrate knowledge from other disciplines?

_____

_____

What culminating sequence will help them consolidate and communicate their learning?

_____

_____

What kind of warm-up, movement exploration, and curriculum connection strategies can lead up to the culminating sequence?

_____

_____

How should they work in the space? What group strategies should they use? sound sources? visual aids?

_____

_____

How can I guide my students to observe and learn from each other's work? How can I guide their reflection process?

_____

_____

It's time to try your lesson. Remember to give yourself time for reflection. These questions might help.

- How did it go?
- What worked?
- What didn't work as well?
- What was a surprise?
- What would I do differently next time?
- Where do my students and I need to go next?
- What help could I use from other teachers, specialists, dance artists, and resources in my community to extend my students' and my own learning in dance?

Chapter 7

Moving into Artistic Expression

In the artistic movement phase, students learn about dance as a performing art. As observers, they investigate different approaches to dance-making. This acquaints them with a wide range of expressive choices. As creators, students are guided by you to make and present their own dances. While they may use curriculum content, they concentrate on communicating what they feel, know, and imagine through movement that they generate, select, structure, and perform.

In this chapter, you will be guided to

- develop an overview of dance
- help students select meaningful content for dances
- guide students' dance-making process
- oversee student presentations.

Creating dances builds on all that you and your students have learned in the natural and creative movement phases. Your students are well versed in movement exploration, have a rich store of movement concepts to draw upon, and have crafted and performed sequences of movement. In some ways the process is more open-ended since students are given time to investigate their ideas and solve creative problems on their own. Yet it is also more defined because they are expected to perform a finished product.

Your role. Offer suggestions for focusing and structuring your students' creative ideas and also give feedback. Remember that rather than engaging in direct instruction, you are mentoring their emergence as young artists. Obviously, younger children will not create highly complex dances. But with your careful guidance, they too can express themselves through dance.

Looking at Dance

Looking at dance, whether in live performance or video, will provide you and your students with a rich context for understanding and making artistic choices. You will see

- what and how dance communicates
- the diversity and power of expression in dance
- the role of music and other sound sources
- theatrical elements such as lighting, costumes, props, and sets.

Creating dances builds on all that you and your students have learned in the natural and creative movement phases.

Do inform your students, however, that they are in no way expected to create at the level of professionals who have dedicated their lives to achieving artistic excellence. Observing dance simply provides knowledge and inspiration.

Understanding Different Dance Forms

As we look at different dance forms, it's worth repeating and remembering that communication is at the heart of dance. I have found it useful to organize dance into four broad categories:

- cultural dance
- representational dance
- presentational dance
- expressive dance.

Cultural. These dances reflect the beliefs, history, geography, customs, ceremonies, and celebrations of different groups of people. Dances from all over the globe—Mexican courtship dances, Appalachian mountain dances, Cambodian classical dance, and the court dances of Ghana—deepen life's meaning for both participants and observers.

Representational. These dances tell stories. It may be a myth expressed in *kathakali* from India, a drama from Japanese *kabuki* theater, or a fairy

Sophiline Cheam Shapiro, photograph by James Wasserman.

tale in classical ballet. The journey and transformation of a character or group of characters is often enacted through this kind of dance. Dances which tell stories are impressions of the story, not literal actions, portrayed through a sequence of expressive movements. As a result, the audience is often prompted to reflect on their own life experiences while experiencing stories through dance.

Presentational. These dances are directed at an audience and are intended to entertain and provide pleasure. Think of a group of skilled tap dancers beating out lively rhythms with their feet. Classical Chinese dancers awe us with their skilled sword play and tumbling moves. Ballet dancers often perform choreography which shows off their ability to move elegantly, balance, jump, and turn. In this kind of dancing, dancers share their virtuosity with us. Through them we feel enlivened and powerful.

Expressive. In these dances, individual artists reflect on the self, life, their heritage, love, compelling characters, the world, music, social issues, and the craft of dancing. Dance elements are made use of in all their expressive potential and structured in original, non-linear ways. The audience makes its own personal connections to the artist's statements on life, the world, or art. We find this kind of creation primarily in modern dance, but also in contemporary ballet, and Japanese *butoh*.

Of course, these dances can and do occupy more than one category. Classical Indian dance expresses spiritual meaning through the stories it tells. The work of screen legends Fred Astaire (1899-1987) and Gene Kelly (1912-1996) reflects these artists' individual views on love and life as much as they entertain. Some consider ballet a form of cultural dance since it originated in the royal courts of sixteenth-century Europe and reflects the values of those people at that time. The categories are simply offered as a tool to help you and your students organize your viewing and understanding.

You may have noticed I have not highlighted social dance. This category includes ballroom, folk, and popular dances. While *Dance as a Way of Knowing* focuses on dance forms which communicate with an audience, social dance forms are in no way considered any less valid to experience and view.

Questions for Viewing

The best way for you and your students to understand more about dance in all its forms is to carefully observe dance at concerts or through video performances. Let's concentrate on how you and your students can learn by watching dance. Asking questions before and/or after students view dance will build on what they already know as movers, creators, and critical thinkers. Asking yourself these questions will also guide your own learning.

What was communicated by the dance? As students respond, point out the common threads, as well as the diversity of their responses. That's exactly as it should be. There is no one right answer when experiencing art. While we may share similar perceptions, we also see things with different perspectives that are shaped by what we've learned and experienced.

Victoria Marks Performance Company, © Lois Greenfield.

What kinds of movements were used in the dance? How was the space used? How did the dance unfold? (If you watched a video, ask these questions, then view the video again.) Students can build on their work as creators and observers to discuss how the dance communicates. You'll probably hear descriptors of Space, Energy, and Time. Students can use the Dance Resource Chart for reference, but bear in mind that the movement concepts listed are fairly rudimentary. Students may generate other more vivid terms to capture what they saw.

Was the dance meaningful and effective? Why or why not? After you validate all responses, tap into students' aesthetic awareness and ask them to describe how the dance did or did not achieve its effectiveness. Ask them to identify parts of the dance that were a surprise or really held their attention. Ask them what they would leave out.

What role did music play in communicating meaning? Ask students to consider the accompanying music or sound sources. Some dance forms, like those from Africa, the Caribbean, and Latin America, cannot be separated from the music that accompanies it. While some modern dances and ballets are made to accompany a piece of music which already exists, we also find that some music is composed especially for a dance. One modern dance choreographer, Merce Cunningham (1922-), decided that dance and music should enjoy equal roles. When he choreographs, the music is created simultaneously. Then the music and dance are put together in performance.

What else contributed to the impact of the dance? Dancers often wear costumes that complement the theme of the dance or symbolize the characters they are portraying. Dramatic lighting adds to the overall expression of the dance, as do props and painted backdrops. Prompting students to consider the impact of music, lighting, costumes, props and backdrops shows them how sound and visuals can support distinctive movements. Even the youngest minds tune in to all aspects of dance production. Many years ago while on tour, I was a member of the Don Redlich Dance Company which gave performances in schools. During a question-and-answer period at one school, a kindergartner asked, "Were your costumes white and colored by the lights, or were your costumes different colors?" (They were different colors.)

S H O P T A L K

The Music Center of Los Angeles. *ARTSOURCE: The Music Center Study Guide to the Performing Arts.* Los Angeles: The Music Center of Los Angeles, 1995.

ARTSOURCE, created and distributed by the Music Center Education Division in Los Angeles, is a useful educational reference guide to the performing arts. Dance, theater, and music units "highlight artists of stature from diverse cultures and a selected work of their art."

Two teacher resource manuals are available for dance. Each contains five units, lesson plans, background information on the artists, as well as video and audio excerpts of selected works. *Artsource-Dance: Cultural Connections* features the work of AMAN Folk Ensemble; American Indian Dance Theater; Amalia Hernandez and Ballet Folklorico de Mexico; Ranganiketan Manipuri Cultural Arts Troupe; and Chuck Davis and the African American Dance Ensemble. *Artsource-Dance: Multidisciplinary Connections* features the work of Alvin Ailey and the Alvin Ailey American Dance Theater; Bella Lewitzky and the Lewitzky Dance Company; Tandy Beal and Bobby McFerrin; Remy Charlip; and Arthur Mitchell and the Dance Theatre of Harlem.

What can we learn by comparing and contrasting different dances? Invite upper elementary students to compare and contrast two different kinds of dances within and between the broad categories of cultural, presentational, representational, and expressive. Sharing their observations will highlight unexpected similarities, and help students appreciate the diversity of dance.

Connecting Your Community to the Dance Community

The best way to look at dance is in live performance. Nothing can take the place of experiencing in person the kinesthetic powers of dancers and the vibrancy they communicate. Having the opportunity to watch a live dance performance, especially after learning about it as a mover and creator, is a very exciting experience. The minute students recognize movements they have experienced, or identify with the ideas expressed in the dance, they connect to dance in a personal way.

Nothing can take the place of experiencing in person the kinesthetic powers of dancers and the vibrancy they communicate.

Dance, like any other discipline, has a community of professionals who practice their craft and seek to share their work with audiences. Some of these artists may live in your town or city, while other dancers are available to travel and visit your school. Your students, as well as your school and community, can develop a relationship with this community of artists. Not only will it extend your students' learning and creativity to observe and work with professionals, but the participation of local and nationally recognized artists will enhance the cultural life of your school and community. Consider

- contacting local dance artists to see if a school performance can be arranged
- contacting the National Assembly of Local Arts Agencies—927 15th Street N.W., Washington, DC 20005—for information on your local arts council which can help you find dance companies with school outreach programs
- arranging a field trip to attend a free dress rehearsal or discounted performance
- sending a letter home to parents asking them to share their expertise in dance
- contacting the dance, world culture, or ethnomusicology departments at your local college or university to see if they offer a performance series (dance students may also be available to offer lecture-demonstrations or performances).

Keep in mind that you always want to seek out dance that demonstrates the highest quality. Just as you direct students to the best sources in literature and research, you will want them to use the highest standards to shape their perceptions of dance. In addition, make sure that the content of the dances is suitable for young audiences. But remember, dance can be of any kind. Just use your aesthetic awareness to help you judge work which is compelling, effective, and might hold the interest of your students.

SHOPTALK

Dance/USA, The National Service Organization for Nonprofit Professional Dance. 1156 15th Street N.W., Suite 820, Washington, DC 20005.

This organization is heading the effort to develop effective collaborations between the dance and educational communities across the United States. Through it, you can contact presenting and arts education organizations, as well as highly regarded dance companies that offer local and national outreach programs. Their large roster of affiliated artists includes: African American Dance Ensemble, Alvin Ailey American Dance Theater, AMAN Folk Ensemble, Ballet Hispanico of New York, Boston Ballet, The Parsons Dance Company, Ririe-Woodbury Dance Company, Paul Taylor Dance Company, and Urban Bush Women.

Video and television. The next best resource for watching dance is video and television. Peruse listings for public television's *Dance In America* and *Great Performances* series, as well as cable arts channels. Watch these shows and tape what you think would be suitable and of interest for your students. Your local video store may stock story ballets, music videos, and first-rate movie musicals like *West Side Story*. Check your library to see if it has the eight-part PBS series *Dancing*.

The Intrinsic Value of Learning about Dance

Regardless of how students learn about dance and apply it to their own efforts, having them learn about different dance forms has intrinsic educational value.

Historical and cultural contexts. Understanding the historical and cultural contexts of dance forms deepens their meaning for students and offers inherent social studies connections. Together you might research

- the culture and historical era the dance form comes from
- why the dance form was originally created
- how the dance form evolved through time
- who or what forces have been the primary catalysts for the evolution of this dance form.

In cultural dances, different groups of people living in diverse regions, with varying economic and religious systems, express their values and beliefs. Students will appreciate different cultures all over the world by learning about their dances. Also, understanding the dances of our own native culture is one way of investigating and maintaining a connection to our heritage.

Studying the history of certain dance forms also acquaints students with how societies have evolved over time. For instance, if students explore the history of tap, jazz, and modern dance, they'll appreciate how different people have contributed to the art and culture of the United States.

Jump Rhythm Jazz Project, photograph by William Frederking.

Literature and drama. Traditional forms of ballet are often based on classic stories like "Giselle," "The Nutcracker," and "A Midsummer's Night Dream." The *bedoyo*, a court dance from Java, tells the story of a sea goddess. The modern dance classic "The Moor's Pavane," by José Limon (1908-1972), is based on *Othello* by William Shakespeare. Watching dances based on stories can acquaint students with the stories themselves and show them how dance can tell stories.

As you will discover in the next section on making dances, expressive dance offers a range of personal, historical, and artistic themes that students can follow into social studies, literature, science, and the arts.

Making Dances

Now that you and your students have an overview of dance, it's time to turn your attention to helping your students make their own dances.

As we investigate the dance-making process together, I offer suggestions for rich content and how to help students structure and perform their material. But I cannot tell you what is going to happen. As their work in the creative movement phase has already demonstrated, dance-making is an open-ended process in which sensitive, imaginative human beings—your students—interact with ideas and movement. The end result is a dance. It is in the doing that dance-making will make the most sense, because that's where you'll see and know how to work with what your students are inventing.

Choosing the Content

When we see a dance, we are experiencing the end product of a long creative process. Like all artists, choreographers usually begin with an idea, image, theme, or event that has meaning for them. This theme is what a dance is "about"—what's being communicated through the movements that are selected and performed.

It is in the doing that dance-making will make the most sense, because that's where you'll see and know how to work with what your students are inventing.

Talk to your students. What content areas hold special interest for them? What kind of dance would they like to make? How could their learning and life experiences become more meaningful by making a dance? You can guide your students to find meaningful ideas to work with from their lives, social issues and historical events, dance, music, visual arts, literature, and curriculum themes.

Life experiences. Students can draw upon life experiences like birthdays, favorite holidays, family, friendship, relocating, growing up, illness, loss, nature, sports, and dreams about the future. Expressive movement often says what words can't capture.

Social issues and historical events. Upper elementary students can explore issues in their own lives or world events. For instance, in the film *West Side Story*, based on Shakespeare's *Romeo and Juliet*, choreographer Jerome Robbins (1918-) conveys masterfully the conflicts that exist between two gangs in New York City in the 1950s. Within the context of their own experiences, or current and historical events, students can focus on the sources of conflicts between groups of people, the choices people make in resolving those conflicts, and the consequences of those choices. Then they can transform their perceptions into a dance.

S H O P T A L K

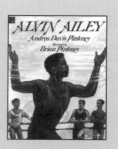

Pinkney, Andrea Davis. *Alvin Ailey*. Illustrated by Brian Pinkney. New York: Hyperion Books, 1993.

Lewis-Ferguson, Julinda. *Alvin Ailey, Jr.: A Life in Dance*. New York: Walker and Company, 1994.

These biographies give children the opportunity to learn about the life and work of modern dance choreographer Alvin Ailey (1931-1989). Mr. Ailey often drew on his personal experiences and African American heritage to create his dances. One of his most acclaimed works, *Revelations*, has touched people all over the world with its universal themes of transcending oppression and celebrating community life.

Alvin Ailey is for younger children. The lively text and illustrations highlight Mr. Ailey's artistic influences during his childhood days in Texas, his student days in Los Angeles, California, where he studied with Lester Horton, and his professional start in New York City.

Alvin Ailey, Jr.: A Life in Dance is for older children. It offers a good description of Mr. Ailey's evolution as an artist, as well as interesting information on the history of modern dance.

Dance. Certain modern dance artists such as Merce Cunningham and Trisha Brown (1936-), focus entirely on the expressive potential of movement and the elements of dance. Students can follow suit and build dances that are based on different kinds of traveling steps, pathways, shapes, energies, and rhythms. Students can also take their inspiration from dances of their own cultural heritage or that of their classmates. The Galef Institute's *History Mysteries* curriculum module has a learning event which invites students to find out about favorite dances and songs within their families. Students can build on this idea as they work in small groups and share these dances with each other. Students can create a group dance which reflects their cultural diversity by learning and combining fragments of each other's dances and songs into a harmonious whole.

Music. Master choreographer George Balanchine (1904-1983), who revolutionized ballet, was inspired by composers as diverse as Tchaikovsky, Stravinsky, Souza, and Gershwin. In African dance, the music often guides the movements of the dancers; cues from the Master Drummer tell the dancers what movements to change to. Our hearts, imaginations, and "moving selves" respond to powerful music like chants, popular songs, symphonic pieces, or drumming music. Students can work imaginatively with music and draw upon their knowledge of the elements of dance to give shape to their responses.

Visual art. Dance artists have not only been inspired by the work of visual artists, but have invited painters and sculptors to create sets and backdrops for their dances. In Chapter 5, you were encouraged to have students connect to the visual arts to deepen their understanding of *shape* in dance movement. They can now use different kinds of visual art—cave paintings, African sculpture, Renaissance art, paintings by Van Gogh, Picasso, Chagall, Jackson Pollack—as a source for an entire dance.

Poetry and literature. Different kinds of poetry, like nursery rhymes, haiku, cinquains, sonnets, and free verse offer students a variety of creative opportunities. So do stories in literature—like *Peter Rabbit* by Beatrix Potter and the *Island of the Blue Dolphins* by Scott O'Dell. Students identify strongly with such books.

Curriculum themes. Any curriculum area may be used as content for dances. Let's look how a community theme can offer students opportunities to communicate what they know, feel, and imagine through dance.

Community. Except for solo artists who choreograph and perform dances by themselves, dance is a communal art form. The dance artist assembles a group of dancers who create, practice, perform, and sometimes travel together on tour for months at a time. The group becomes a community as it focuses on achieving something larger than themselves—a clear, strong, expressive presentation of the dances. Communities across the curriculum provide rich areas of exploration for your students.

Ecological communities. Throughout time, poets, composers, visual artists, choreographers, and photographers have drawn inspiration from nature. Students can build on their work with animals in Chapter 4 and their "geography journey" in Chapter 5 to create dances based on different ecosystems.

Historical communities. Students can create

- ceremonies of Egyptian pharaohs and their followers to ensure that the Nile flooded and made the soil fertile
- a dance based on Olympic events in ancient Greece such as the long jump, the javelin throw, and the discus
- a dance which communicates the essence of what they know about the life of children in the Colonies—a composite of movements based on family life, work, schooling, and play.

Field Notes: Teacher-To-Teacher

During our study of the Northwest Coast Kwakiutl tribe, small groups investigated the areas of shelter, clothing, foods, ceremonies and art design. As a culminating activity, we hosted a Potlatch ceremony, raising the totem pole constructed by the class, and students presented their projects. Several groups performed dance sequences to portray building a longhouse, making clothes from cedar bark, catching and preparing salmon, and constructing totem poles and canoes. Rounding out the experience, others used instruments to add beat and rhythm.

Pam Strain
Emma W. Shuey Elementary School
Rosemead, California

While some students' dances may flower organically as they work, other students may benefit from having guidelines that help determine how their dances will unfold.

Choosing a Structure

While some students' dances may flower organically as they work, other students may benefit from having guidelines that help determine how their dances will unfold. A loose structure provides a way to begin, develop, and conclude a dance. It's an expanded version of the culminating sequence your students have experienced throughout *Dance as a Way of Knowing*.

Here are some examples of guidelines you and your students can create together. Students can

- assemble ten different kinds of walks
- enter the space and introduce a theme for thirty-two beats (or four sets of eight beats); vary the theme by integrating the elements of dance in three different ways for forty-eight beats; bring the dance to a resolution, either in place or by exiting in thirty-two beats
- use the embedded sequence of a journey, a story, a scientific process, a piece of music or song, for example, as the structure for a dance.

Getting to Work

Once the objectives and guidelines have been established, it's time to turn the project over to your students. If they've progressed through all the phases of the movement and dance learning continuum, most should have no trouble expanding into the challenges and joys of making dances.

DIALOGUE

What are my objectives? What do I want my students to know and be able to do at the end of this experience?

_____

_____

What group strategies do I feel comfortable inviting my students to use?

_____

_____

How much time will my students have to plan, explore, make, rehearse, and present their dances. Will they have several weeks? a few months? the whole school year? (Remember, the less time they have, the more limited their objectives should be.)

_____

_____

Will my students share their dances with each other in the classroom? with the rest of the school in a multi-purpose room? with families and schoolmates on a lighted stage?

_____

_____

Here are some ways to help them step into this new creative territory. With your help, students can

- develop criteria for their dance
- identify the movement concepts they can work with
- reflect on their ideas and experiences in their dance journals through writing and drawing whenever they come up with ideas for their dance
- take time to explore and solve creative problems—time will enable them to move beyond superficial choices, and dig deeply
- solve the problems in motion—the movements students generate will give them new ideas and tell them where to go next in ways that sitting around and thinking won't

- show their work at regular intervals to get feedback from you and classmates
- establish clear beginnings and endings for their dances.

At this point, your role is to help them stay on task and offer suggestions if they come to you with questions. Unless you are guiding a whole group of younger students to create a dance together, let your students become accustomed to exploring their movement ideas without you.

SHOPTALK

Humphrey, Doris. *The Art of Making Dances.* New York: Grove Weidenfeld, 1991.

Doris Humphrey was a modern dance pioneer, renowned teacher, and mentor to many dance artists. First published in 1958, this book is a clear presentation of the principles underlying her approach to modern dance choreography. The way she works with Space, Energy, and Time (which she calls "the design, dynamics, and rhythm of dance") will deepen your understanding of the dance-making process.

THE ART OF MAKING DANCES

BY DORIS HUMPHREY

Music, Costumes, Props, Backdrops

As their work proceeds, ask students to think about what their dances need in the way of sound accompaniment (if students are not already working with music), costumes, and props. If students need to support their work with taped music or other sound sources, be prepared to give them some sug-

gestions. If several groups are using taped music, you may need to gather some extra cassette recorders so they can practice with music. Encourage students to use original, live sound sources like voices and percussion instruments.

Ask everyone to start thinking about simple costume ideas that are easy to assemble, add distinction to the dances, and allow students to move easily. You might try

- long, colorful T-shirts over black tights or pants
- scarves or sashes made out of brightly colored, or patterned material
- collars and gloves.

What about props? Because props can inhibit motion, they should only be used if they add significantly to the impact of the dance. Since students are moving, it is of utmost importance that props be entirely safe. Prohibit anything with a sharp point or edges and avoid props that have several parts or are breakable. If working on a stage, consider using a painted backdrop, projected images, as well as lighting to support the theme of the dance.

After students have enjoyed another work period in which they have revised their dances again and have integrated these other theatrical elements, they are ready to focus on presenting their dances. Arts education author and consultant Jane Remer suggests having your class form a dance company. (Make it a company of peers with its very own name; you can be the general manager.) The dance company can attend to all the "business" of presenting a performance—posting and sending out written notices (publicity), gathering and organizing costumes and props, and setting up the performing and viewing areas. This connection to real-life experience will help students understand the hard work that goes into preparing for public performances.

Preparing for Performance

Performing a dance is one of the few times in life where you invest your body, heart, mind, and spirit all at once. Instead of using words, we communicate feelings, facts, impressions, and insights to another group of human beings through defined, expressive movements.

It takes profound concentration to channel all your physical, emotional, and creative energy in this fashion. Whatever your students' performance venue— the classroom, a multi-purpose room, or even on a brightly lit stage—they'll need to practice, or, as it is known in the performing arts, time to "rehearse." This may start out as a way for students to remember what they've created, but as the performance draws near, rehearsal should be a time for students to focus on performing the movements as clearly, fully, and expressively as possible. You can guide even the youngest of students to think of "speaking" to an audience while dancing. If their movements are fuzzy or muted, ask them to imagine that the audience is sitting very far away, and that they need to send their movements to the very back row.

Another reason for having students practice as much as possible is to offset the impact of having an audience. The more the dance movements have settled in your students' muscles, the less likely they'll be distracted by having an audience. If possible, invite another class to view your class's dances before the official performance. This will acquaint your students with what it feels like to dance while a group of human beings watches them attentively. (If this is a new experience for both the performers and observers, make sure the class that is watching has gone over guidelines for being a good audience.)

Encourage your students to stay focused on their dancing and what they're supposed to be doing with fellow dancers—not on anything else. If, during a run-through, a few things go wrong, establish the cardinal rule of live performing: "Keep going no matter what."

A dance invites an audience into a special realm. It's a realm filled with physical power and personal feeling. If someone stops the energy, the bond with the audience is broken. So encourage students to keep going even if they forget a move or go in the wrong direction. Tell them to stay focused, make something up on the spot, and get back in sync as soon as possible. No one in the audience knows what's supposed to happen.

The bow. Be sure to organize a bow for the end of the performance. A bow gives performers the opportunity to thank the audience for its attention and the audience a chance to thank the dancers for their performance. Have students stand shoulder to shoulder across the performing space looking out at the audience, then follow whomever is standing in the middle as she or he bows and straightens.

The Performance

The moment has arrived! Whether it's an informal showing in your classroom or on a stage, the minute the music begins or the first movers set foot on stage, that unique form of communication known as dance takes over. Your students share what they know and care about with their audience through movements they have created and now bring fully to life.

Reflection

After the performance, give the whole class the opportunity to reflect on all that they have learned, experienced, and felt while making and presenting their dances. If the performance was videotaped, view it together so everyone can bask in a sense of accomplishment together and acknowledge each other's work. Then ask students to reflect in their dance journals.

Dance Journal

Making the dance was _____

_____

Why? _____

_____

_____

Performing the dance was _____

_____

Making the dance reminded me of _____

_____

Making and performing the dance helped me to _____

_____

The next time I make a dance, I would like _____

_____

Portrait of a Skilled, Artistic Mover

In the artistic movement phase, students' participation in the creation and performance of dances is evidence that they have internalized the knowledge they developed in the natural movement and creative movement phases. Let's take a closer look.

Participation. The student is able to work on his or her own, with a partner, in a trio, or in a group as a collaborative problem-solver; can select content and structure for a dance on his or her own, in collaboration with you or classmates (depending on age and movement and dance experience); and can present his or her dance to an audience.

Movement. The student is able to fulfill the demands of different parts of the artistic process by working with content/theme and structure; and can explore, generate, select, assess, revise, and sequence movement choices into a repeatable, artistic whole.

Aesthetic Awareness. *As a mover/creator:* The student moves in full-bodied, expressive ways with energy, clarity, fluidity, and skill. The student creates sequences out of movements of various sizes, levels, speeds, force, weight, quality, rhythms, and patterns; and is able to create a compelling, meaningful whole.

As an observer: The student is able to articulate what is being communicated in a dance, how meaning is communicated, what else contributes to the impact of a dance and whether and how the dance was effective.

The Finale

For most people, learning about movement and dance takes them into uncharted territory. Since you started off by moving your hands, and ended up guiding the creation and performance of your students' dances, it's clear you have traveled a great distance. You have acknowledged your students as movers, learners, explorers and inventors. In so doing, you have enhanced their lives. You have contributed to the art of teaching by carving a trail for fellow educators who may want to channel their students' abundant energy but don't know where to start.

Your students have learned new ways to investigate, make choices, work together, communicate, and make connections. They know how to honor their imaginations, work hard, and put their visions into motion. These are abilities that serve them well now as elementary school students, and you can take pride and pleasure in knowing that these newly developed abilities will continue to guide your students' learning and thinking for the rest of their lives.

Professional Bibliography

Bridges, Lois. *Assessment: Continuous Learning*. Strategies for Teaching and Learning Professional Library, The Galef Institute. York, Maine: Stenhouse Publishers, 1995.

————. *Creating Your Classroom Community*. Strategies for Teaching and Learning Professional Library, The Galef Institute. York, Maine: Stenhouse Publishers, 1995.

Calais-Germain, Blandine. *Anatomy of Movement*. Seattle: Eastland Press, 1993.

Cambigue, Susan. *Learning through Dance Movement*. Los Angeles: Performing Tree, 1981.

Cohen, Selma Jeanne. *Dance as a Theatre Art: Source Readings in Dance History from 1581 to the Present*. Pennington, New Jersey: Princeton Book Company, 1992.

Consortium of National Arts Education Associations. *National Standards for Arts Education*. Reston, Virginia: Music Educators National Conference, 1994.

Copeland, Roger and Marshall Cohen, ed. *What Is Dance?: Readings in Theory and Criticism*. New York: Oxford University Press, 1983.

Csikszentmihalyi, Mihaly. *The Evolving Self: A Psychology for the Third Millennium*. New York: HarperCollins, 1993.

Dance Films Association. *Dance Film and Video Guide,* compiled by Deirdre Towers. Pennington, New Jersey: Princeton Book Company, 1991.

De Mille, Agnes. *Dance to the Piper.* Boston: Little, Brown, 1952.

Emery, Lynne Fauley. *Black Dance: From 1619 to Today.* Pennington, New Jersey: Princeton Book Company, 1988.

Fitzhenry, Robert I., ed. *The Harper Book of Quotations.* 3rd ed. New York: HarperPerennial, 1993.

Galef Institute. *History Mysteries: Discovering the Past.* Los Angeles: Galef Institute, 1994.

Gardner, Howard. *Creating Minds: An Anatomy of Creativity Seen through the Lives of Freud, Einstein, Picasso, Stravinsky, Eliot, Graham, and Gandhi.* New York: BasicBooks, 1993.

———. *Frames of Mind: The Theory of Multiple Intelligences.* New York: BasicBooks, 1983.

Grant, Janet Millar. *Shake, Rattle, and Learn: Classroom-tested Ideas that Use Movement for Active Learning.* York, Maine: Stenhouse Publishers, 1995; Markham, Ontario: Pembroke Publishers, 1995.

Hart, Mickey with Jay Stevens and Frederic Lieberman. *Drumming at the Edge of Magic.* New York: HarperCollins, 1990.

H'Doubler, Margaret N. *Dance: A Creative Art Experience.* Madison, Wisconsin: The University of Wisconsin Press, 1957.

Heller, Paul G. *Drama as a Way of Knowing.* Strategies for Teaching and Learning Professional Library, The Galef Institute. York, Maine: Stenhouse Publishers, 1995.

Highwater, Jamake. *Dance: Rituals of Experience.* 3rd ed. New York: Oxford University Press, 1996.

Humphrey, Doris. *The Art of Making Dances.* New York: Grove Weidenfeld, 1991.

Jonas, Gerald. *Dancing: The Pleasure, Power, and Art of Movement.* New York: Harry N. Abrams in association with Thirteen/WNET, 1992.

Joyce, Mary. *First Steps in Teaching Creative Dance to Children.* 2nd ed. Mountain View, California: Mayfield Publishing Company, 1980.

———. *Dance Technique for Children.* Palo Alto, California: Mayfield Publishing Company, 1984.

Laban, Rudolf. *Modern Educational Dance.* 3rd ed. London: MacDonald and Evans, 1975.

Levine, Mindy N. *Widening the Circle: Towards a New Vision for Dance Education.* Washington, D.C.: Dance/USA, 1994.

Martinello, Marian L. and Gillian E. Cook, "The Interdisciplinary Qualities of Inquiry," *Educational Forum*, Fall 1993.

Murray, Ruth Lovell. *Dance in Elementary School Education.* 3rd ed. New York: Harper and Row, 1975.

The Music Center of Los Angeles County. *ARTSOURCE: The Music Center Study Guide to the Performing Arts.* Los Angeles: The Music Center of Los Angeles County, 1995.

Ohanian, Susan. *Math as a Way of Knowing.* Strategies for Teaching and Learning Professional Library, The Galef Institute. York, Maine: Stenhouse Publishers, 1995.

Page, Nick. *Music as a Way of Knowing.* Strategies for Teaching and Learning Professional Library, The Galef Institute. York, Maine: Stenhouse Publishers, 1995.

Smith-Autard, Jacqueline M. *The Art of Dance in Education.* London: A and C Black, 1994.

The Stonesong Press. *The New York Public Library Performing Arts Desk Reference.* New York: MacMillan, 1994.

Turner, Margery J. *New Dance: Approaches to Non-literal Choreography.* Pittsburgh: University of Pittsburgh Press, 1971.

Visual and Performing Arts Framework for California Public Schools. Sacramento, California: California Department of Education, 1996.

von Oech, Roger. *A Whack on the Side of the Head: How You Can Be Creative.* Illustrated by George Willett. Menlo Park, California: Creative Think, 1992.

Warner, Sylvia Ashton. *Teacher.* New York: Bantam Books, 1995.

Wigman, Mary. *The Language of Dance.* Translated from the German by Walter Sorrell. Middletown, Connecticut: Wesleyan University, 1966.

Videos

Dancing. New York: Thirteen/WNET, RM Arts and BBC-TV, 1993.

Exploring Curriculum Ideas Through Dance. Los Angeles: Performing Tree, 1985.

West Side Story. Los Angeles: United Artists, 1961.

Music

Ade, King Sunny and His African Beats. *Juju Music.* New York: Mango Records, 1982.

Gipsy Kings. *The Best of the Gipsy Kings.* New York: Nonesuch Records, 1995.

Olatunji, Babatunde. *Olatunji! Drums of Passion.* New York: Columbia Records, 1990.

Dvořák, Anton. *Symphony No. 9* ("New World"). Hackensack, New Jersey: Essex Entertainment, 1990.

Bream, Julian. *Baroque Guitar.* New York: BMG Music, 1990.

Deuter, Chitanya Hari. *Cicada.* Tucson, Arizona: Celestial Harmonies, 1982.

Enya. *Shepherd Moons.* Burbank, California: Reprise Records, 1991.

Kater, Peter and R. Carlos Nakai. *Migration.* Boulder, Colorado: Silver Wave Records, 1992.

Nakai, R. Carlos. *Emergence: Songs of the Rainbow World.* Phoenix: Canyon Records Productions, 1992.

Roach, Steve. *Structures from Silence.* Tucson, Arizona: Celestial Harmonies, 1984.

Roth, Gabrielle and the Mirrors. *Initiation.* Red Bank, New Jersey: Raven Recording, 1988.

Whitesides-Woo, Rob. *Mountain Light.* Mariastein, Ohio: Serenity, 1992.

Children's Bibliography

Ávila, Victoria. *How Our Muscles Work*. Illustrated by Antonio Muñoz Tenllado. New York: Chelsea House, 1995. For upper elementary students—an in-depth look at how muscles operate throughout the human body.

Carle, Eric. *From Head to Toe*. New York: HarperCollins, 1997. In Carle's distinctive and engaging illustrations, animals invite children to move in a variety of ways. This book can help primary grade students learn how to listen and put verbal prompts into motion.

Cohn, Amy L., ed. *From Sea to Shining Sea: A Treasury of American Folklore and Folk Songs*. New York: Scholastic, 1993. A collection of songs and stories from cultures that have contributed to the rich fabric of American life.

Fleischman, Paul. *Rondo in C*. Illustrated by Janet Wentworth. New York: Harper and Row, 1988. This picture book captures the imaginative responses of different individuals as they listen to Beethoven's Rondo in C during a piano recital.

Garfunkel, Trudy. *Letter to the World: The Life and Dances of Martha Graham*. Boston: Little, Brown, 1995. A biography, for upper elementary students, of the woman credited by many with establishing modern dance as an art form.

Gray, Libba Moore. *My Mama Had a Dancing Heart*. Illustrated by Raul Colon. New York: Orchard Books, 1995. A young girl's warm-hearted, lively dance through the seasons.

Hoyt-Goldsmith, Diane. *Totem Pole*. Photographs by Lawrence Migdale. New York: Holiday House, 1990. Depicts the true-life creation of a Native American totem, as well as a community's celebration of its installation, as seen through the eyes of the totem carver's son.

Hughes, Langston. *The Book of Rhythms*. New York: Oxford University Press, 1995. A lyrical meditation on the rhythms that exist in nature, culture, and everyday life.

Krull, Kathleen. *Wilma Unlimited*. Illustrated by David Diaz. San Diego: Harcourt Brace, 1996. A portrait of famed athlete Wilma Rudolph—for primary grades.

Lambert, David. *The Children's Animal Atlas*. Brookfield, Connecticut: The Millbrook Press, 1992. Detailed, well-presented information about animals and their habitats.

Lewis-Ferguson, Julinda. *Alvin Ailey, Jr.: A Life in Dance*. New York: Walker and Company, 1994. For older children, this biography traces the artistic evolution of an esteemed modern dance choreographer.

Lionni, Leo. *Swimmy*. New York: Pantheon Books, 1968. The wonderfully illustrated journey of a resourceful, orphaned fish—for primary grades.

Liptak, Karen. *North American Indian Sign Language*. New York: Franklin Watts, 1990. An illustrated resource for learning Native American Sign Language.

Locker, Thomas. *Water Dance*. San Diego: Harcourt Brace, 1997. A poetic, colorful illustrated look at water as it dances through life on earth. Includes scientific information on the water cycle (by Candace Christiansen) in the back of the book.

Marshak, Suzanna. *I Am the Ocean*. Illustrated by James Endicott. Boston: Little, Brown, 1991. The poetic text and fine illustrations capture the complexity of ocean life.

McGovern, Ann. *...If You Lived in Colonial Times*. Illustrated by June Otani. New York: Scholastic, 1992. An informative look, for primary grades, at the life of early American settlers.

O'Dell, Scott. *Island of the Blue Dolphins*. Boston: Houghton Mifflin, 1960. The compelling story, for upper elementary students, of a resourceful child who survives by herself on an island.

Potter, Beatrix. *The Tale of Peter Rabbit*. New York: Warner Books, 1988. The classic story of an adventurous bunny who gets into and out of trouble.

Pinkney, Andrea Davis. *Alvin Ailey*. Illustrated by Brian Pinkney. New York: Hyperion Books, 1993. This biography for primary grades describes the childhood influences and early artistry of a major modern dance choreographer.

Raschka, Chris. *Charlie Parker Played Be Bop*. New York: Orchard Books, 1992. This jazz poem celebrates a well-known saxophonist through rhythmical words which dance across bold illustrations.

Seuss, Dr. *Oh, The Places You'll Go!* New York: Random House, 1990. A delightfully unpredictable journey through life for primary and mid-elementary students.

Silverstein, Shel. *Where the Sidewalk Ends*. New York: Harper and Row, 1974. A collection of lively, often humorous poems for upper elementary students.

Surat, Michele Maria. *Angel Child, Dragon Child*. Illustrated by Vo-Dinh Mai. New York: Scholastic, 1983. A sensitive portrayal—for primary grades—of a Vietnamese child settling into her life in America.

Taylor, Barbara. *Maps and Mapping*. New York: Kingfisher Books, 1993. Concise information on the function and creation of maps.

Venezia, Mike. *Picasso*. Chicago: Children's Press, 1988. A refreshing yet substantive look at the life and work of a major European visual artist. This book—like those on artists such as Diego Rivera and Georgia O'Keefe—appeals to kids and preserves the integrity of the artist.

Walker, Richard. *The Children's Atlas of the Human Body*. Brookfield, Connecticut: The Millbrook Press, 1994. Detailed descriptions of the major systems of the human body—for upper elementary students.

Wilson, Forrest. *What It Feels Like To Be a Building*. Washington, D.C.: The Preservation Press, 1988. Action words and clever illustrations offer older students a unique way to understand architectural forces through kinesthetic imagery.

Yashima, Taro. *Crow Boy*. New York: Puffin Books, 1983. The moving tale of a young boy whose unique relationship to life is demeaned, then is valued by his schoolmates—thanks to the intervention of his teacher.

Yenawine, Philip. *Lines*. New York: Delacorte Press, 1991.

———. Shapes. New York: Delacorte Press, 1991. The author explicates the visual arts concepts of "line" and "shape" by looking at the work of well-known artists.

Professional Associations and Publications

The American Alliance for Health, Physical
Education, Recreation, and Dance
(AAHPERD)
*Journal of Physical Education, Recreation,
and Dance*
1900 Association Drive
Reston, Virginia 22091

American Alliance for Theater and Education
(AATE)
AATE Newsletter
c/o Arizona State University Theater Department
Box 873411
Tempe, Arizona 85287

American Association for the Advancement
of Science (AAAS)
Science Magazine
1333 H Street NW
Washington, DC 20005

American Association of Colleges for Teacher
Education (AACTE)
AACTE Briefs
1 DuPont Circle NW, Suite 610
Washington, DC 20036

American Association of School Administrators
(AASA)
The School Administrator
1801 North Moore Street
Arlington, Virginia 22209

Association for Childhood Education
International (ACEI)
*Childhood Education: Infancy Through
Early Adolescence*
11141 Georgia Avenue, Suite 200
Wheaton, Maryland 20902

Association for Supervision and Curriculum
Development (ASCD)
Educational Leadership
1250 North Pitt Street
Alexandria, Virginia 22314

The Council for Exceptional Children (CEC)
Teaching Exceptional Children
1920 Association Drive
Reston, Virginia 22091

Education Theater Association (ETA)
Dramatics
3368 Central Parkway
Cincinnati, Ohio 45225

International Reading Association
(IRA)
The Reading Teacher
800 Barksdale Road
Newark, Delaware 19714

Music Educators National Conference
(MENC)
Music Educators Journal
1806 Robert Fulton Drive
Reston, Virginia 22091

National Art Education Association
(NAEA)
Art Education
1916 Association Drive
Reston, Virginia 22091

National Association for the Education
of Young Children (NAEYC)
Young Children
1509 16th Street NW
Washington, DC 20036

National Association of Elementary
School Principals (NAESP)
Communicator
1615 Duke Street
Alexandria, Virginia 22314

National Center for Restructuring
Education, Schools, and Teaching
(NCREST)
Resources for Restructuring
P.O. Box 110
Teachers College, Columbia University
New York, New York 10027

National Council for the Social Studies
(NCSS)
Social Education
Social Studies and the Young Learner
3501 Newark Street NW
Washington, DC 20016

National Council of Supervisors of
Mathematics (NCSM)
NCSM Newsletter Leadership in
Mathematics Education
P.O. Box 10667
Golden, Colorado 80401

National Council of Teachers of
English (NCTE)
Language Arts
Primary Voices K-6
1111 Kenyon Road
Urbana, Illinois 61801

National Council of Teachers of
Mathematics (NCTM)
Arithmetic Teacher
Teaching Children Mathematics
1906 Association Drive
Reston, Virginia 22091

National Dance Association
(NDA)
Spotlight on Dance
1900 Association Drive
Reston, Virginia 22091

National Science Teachers Association
(NSTA)
Science and Children
Science for Children: Resources for Teachers
1840 Wilson Boulevard
Arlington, Virginia 22201

Phi Delta Kappa
Phi Delta Kappan
408 North Union
Bloomington, Indiana 47402

Society for Research in Music Education
Journal for Research in Music Education
c/o Music Educators National Conference
1806 Robert Fulton Drive
Reston, Virginia 22091

The Southern Poverty Law Center
Teaching Tolerance
400 Washington Avenue
Montgomery, Alabama 36104

Teachers of English to Speakers of Other
Languages (TESOL)
TESOL Newsletter
1600 Cameron Street, Suite 300
Alexandria, Virginia 22314